Antarctica is the highest, driest, windiest, coldest, most remote, inhospitable and unforgiving place on the planet. The temperature at the South Pole reaches 90 degrees below zero. Antarctica is a place full of hazards, unknowns, constant changes and non-stop threats.

That's an accurate description of the business world today, isn't it? Every day we are faced with threats, changes, obstacles and unpredictable factors that come without warning—making business success and survival difficult.

The key to success in Antarctica, and in your business, is preparation. You are on an expedition. An exciting, challenging and important expedition. Your goal is meaningful work and success. If you, your team, and your company are going to thrive—much less survive—you have to be prepared. You have to plan as carefully as the Polar explorers did 100 years ago.

Welcome to a new way of looking at leadership and business. It's different. It's exhilarating. I'd like to help you to conquer your own Antarctica.

Antarctic Publishing

LEADING
AT 90 BELOW ZERO

[Extreme Conditions...Extraordinary Results]

FIRST EDITION

Antarctic Mike

TABLE OF CONTENTS

"Everyone has an Antarctica to conquer. What's yours?"

— ANTARCTIC MIKE

EVERY DAY WE ALL BATTLE "THE ELEMENTS"

The elements in Antarctica are a constant threat and hazard. The ice covering the entire continent averages more than one mile in thickness, and is littered with crevasses that can swallow entire teams of people. Every day there are hurricane force winds, whiteout blizzards, and in the winter, months of complete darkness. Oh, and don't forget the chilly conditions. The average temperature at the South Pole year-round is 58 degrees below zero, Fahrenheit. And it occasionally plunges to 90 degrees below zero—thus the title of this book.

Antarctica is the most challenging environment on earth. There are similar hazards in the real world, making success difficult, and sometimes impossible, to attain.

If you and your company are going to get ahead—and stay ahead—you're going to have to plan and be prepared for your expedition in ways that are levels above where you are today. Think about how much competition there is for new business; how challanging it is to find and keep great talent; and how many unpredictable circumstances will make your journey hazardous.

The key comes down to one thing: Are you ready to lead the expedition? Really ready? Do you know how to condition and prepare your people to conquer their own Antarctica on a continuous basis? This book is designed to tell you what you need to *know* and what you need to *do* in order to find, engage and keep the best performing people. The very best companies do just this, no matter what the conditions. The principles in *Leading at 90 Below Zero* will help you and your team do just that.

WHY ANTARCTICA?

In 2006, I was one of just nine people to run in the first ever Antarctic Ice Marathon. That's right, a full 26.2-mile marathon run on an ice shelf located a mere 600 miles from the South Pole. This was the first marathon I had run in more than 20 years, and only the second of my life, let alone in Antarctica.

If you're like most people, you're asking, "Why?" The irony is that my reasons for participating had little to do with running, sports or cold weather. Rather, it was about following in the footsteps of my Polar hero, the man who really put Antarctica on the map more than 100 years ago.

You ask, "Why would you want to follow in the steps of your Polar hero?" The answer is simple: The men who first conquered the ends of the earth were some of the best leaders the world has ever seen. And of them, one man stands head-and-shoulders above the rest: Ernest Shackleton.

Shackleton's ability to lead his team members through tremendous difficulties is legendary—and it's what drew me to him and his stories. My purpose in following in the footsteps of the greatest Polar explorer—widely acknowledged as one of the greatest leaders in history—is to help you be more effective in your abilities to lead your people, your customers, and others.

Every single person, every day, is called to be a great leader. Every conversation, text message, email, interchange or conversation is an opportunity to lead effectively. Regardless of your age, job title, years of experience, or any other factor, the truth is that all of us are leading someone. The question is this: How effective are you as a leader?

An expedition is simply a journey for an intended purpose. This is exactly what teams do today—whether they are business teams, soccer teams, social teams or church teams—and they have a specific purpose.

The early Polar explorers intentionally went into conditions that were somewhere between difficult and dangerous—many for the first time ever. Along the way from point A to point B there were obstacles, opportunities, hazards, and many unknowns. This is exactly what teams in the real world experience every day. Companies and organizations start at one point and are trying to go to new destinations for a defined purpose. Along the way, there are opportunities, obstacles, hazards, and many other challenges similar to those that were faced by the early Antarctic explorers.

The important questions are: Are you prepared? Is your team ready? Are they conditioned properly to get from point A to point B…knowing that they will face challenges that will take them on a zig-zag course through C, D, Q and probably X. Will they be able to seize the opportunities they set out to find? Will they be able to respond to the changes that will so quickly come upon them? Will they be able to zig and zag when circumstances call for such moves? Will they be able to stay the course, mentally and physically?

> *"Success is a destination between difficult and dangerous."*
> — ANTARCTIC MIKE

Whether you are conquering harsh conditions like in Antarctica, or you work for a company today, the challenges and difficulties you face are the same. The only difference is that the elements in the Antarctic are obvious and pronounced. In the real world, the elements blend in with everything around you, so they appear to be normal. However, damage is still being done, and many people don't realize it. Will you not only survive, but thrive? Knowing what to do in order to prepare and execute properly is what great leaders do.

Welcome to *Leading at 90 Below Zero*.

In my opinion Ernest Shackleton was the poster child of a great leader. More specifically, it was his character that was the draw. I find it incredibly inspiring to read about people who intentionally take on new challenges and who live to *create* history, instead of riding on the coattails of others.

This is exactly what attracts and engages the best performing people today. They want to be part of a team that is creating history and changing people's lives. They want to be fully employed and fully engaged. They want to try new things, take risks and push themselves in ways they never thought possible.

This is exactly what the Polar pioneers did. And this is why Shackleton is such a great role model for us to learn from.

Now you may be saying, "Not everyone on my team thinks like that. I have plenty of people who *don't* want to be challenged and pushed. They just want to show up, do the minimum and collect a check before disappearing." I agree with you on this point. It supports the research that indicates that only one in five employees is consistently engaged. One in five! An important question is, "Why are these people like this?" More importantly, as a leader you have to ask yourself, "What *can* I do, and what *will* I do about this?"

If the employees driving your business aren't continuously taking on new challenges and pushing the bar higher, the question is, "What is the impact on your entire organization, your customers, your reputation and your future pool of employees and new customers?" The answer is, "*A lot more than you may realize!*" What can you personally do to address this?

Leading at 90 Below Zero is all about leadership, and about specific actions that you can take to address the issues related to finding, engaging and keeping the best people. That's what great leaders have always done... and it's what they do today. When I say "best people" I'm referring not only to employees but to customers, too. The leadership principles that will attract and keep better employees are the same principles that will attract and keep better customers (and I'm defining "better customer" as the person who will drive a mile further, and pay a dollar more, for a like item or service.) That's what I will help you master.

Great leadership is not an easy expedition. It will push you further than you've been pushed before. It will call you to places you've never gone to—places that are unfamiliar, challenging, and sometimes outright frightening. It will require a level of discipline and commitment beyond what you've ever achieved. It will push you, test you and reveal to you what you're really made of. For those who are willing and able to go those distances, and to those places, the impact is endless and the rewards are priceless. Welcome to *Leading at 90 Below Zero*.

Sometimes you have to go too far in order to know how far you really can go

WHERE IT ALL STARTED

Once upon a time . . . There was an eighth grader who looked at the pull-down map of the world at the front of the classroom. It was Mr. Hammer's social studies class at Salisbury Middle School, in Allentown, Pennsylvania. As that boy stared at the wall map of the world, his eyes were fixed on the mass of white at the very bottom of the earth. What was that? Why weren't there any cities, roads, or anything else on the entire continent? I was fascinated and mystified.

I asked myself, "What would this place look like? Why would people go there? What would they learn?" And most importantly, "What would they learn and bring back to the real world?" Little did I know that at ths moment a seed was planted in my mind and heart that would change my life—and the lives of many others—decades later.

Thus began my journey that would eventually take me to Antarctica-twice! Once, to be one of the first nine people in history to run a marathon on the frozen continent, and once to run a 100-kilometer Ultra Marathon.

Back in Mr. Hammer's class. . . I was drawn to that map of the world. It dramatically covered the entire wall. I remember the kids gathering around and exclaiming, "There's New York City, where the Yankees play." or

"There's Paris, home of the Eiffel Tower!" or "There's Los Angeles and Hollywood!"

I just stood there and whispered, "There's Ant-arctica." I remember staring at that map and reading "The Ross Ice Shelf." I tried as hard as I could to imagine an ice shelf a thousand miles across. I couldn't do it.

That's when and where my Antarctic story started—back in Salisbury Middle school in Allentown, Pennsylvania; it then continued at the University of Colorado in Boulder; then to a Barnes & Noble bookstore in Bakersfield, California; then to hundreds of cities around the world; then to a warehouse freezer in San Diego; then to Antarctica…and finally to **YOU**, the person who's reading my story. My goal is to inspire **YOU** to be a better leader through the story of Ernest Shackleton and what I learned by walking in his footsteps. I wanted to get a small taste of what he and his team experienced over 100 years ago, and bring those lessons learned to you. Those men survived in conditions that were as extreme as any team has ever faced. They were successful largely in part because of the leadership of Ernest Shackleton-the most famous of the early Antarctic explorers and one of the greatest leaders who ever lived. That's why I ran a marathon and returned to run an ultra marathon in Antarctica.

And all of this was to walk in the shoes of my hero—Ernest Shackleton—the most famous of the early Antarctic explorers and one of the greatest leaders who ever lived.

GETTING THE MOST FROM THIS BOOK

In order to make your time count, here's how you'll get the most out of my book. As you proceed through the story, set a goal to walk away with one solid conviction...

That's "*One* solid conviction." One. Not ten. Choose just one that resonates with you. One that you will actually act on.

> *"A goal is a dream with a plan and a deadline."*
>
> — HARVEY MACKAY

I'm going share a lot of stories and ideas with you. I think they're *all* great ideas and principles that you can use. But I've learned that different people need different ideas at different times in their lives. The ideas are going to demonstrate solid characteristics of leadership, evidenced by stories from Antarctica. As you proceed, I want you to identify one point that really resonates with you. Think about how it fits into *your* world, why it's important to *you*, and what you'll *do* with it.

Taking action on something specific, and under-standing why it's important to you and your team, are critically important. *Internally*, you'll be inspired, and *externally*, you'll change your actions, which will change your results.

And let me clarify one important point: The "con-viction" part of "One solid conviction" includes a specific plan of action. Ideas by themselves are a dime-a-dozen, but ideas connected to *action plans* are worth a million bucks!

INSPIRED!

Okay, back to school we go, to the University of Colorado. I wasn't a particularly academic kind of guy. I like my knowledge at a first grade level, meaning simple and straight forward. When I entered the University, I had to pick a major. I looked through the course catalog and read: Sociology, Psychology, Math, English—and when I came to Engineering, my instant thought was, "Heck! I don't want to be a train conductor for the rest of my life!" This tells you that I'm not exactly the poster child for being a school guy.

I walked away with a business degree. In addition, I learned two important lessons that changed my life. First, the importance of great stories, and second, a love of speaking-speaking to groups; speaking with purpose; speaking with passion. It was in college that I discovered my talent and interest of being a speaker. And I mean speaking to a group of people. Speaking with a purpose. Speaking with passion.

In 1983, during my freshman year, I attended a Christian seminar that included several inspirational speakers. One of them changed my life. His name was Tom Brown. He could engage a crowd and tell stories unlike anyone I've ever heard—then or since. I knew that very day that I wanted to be a speaker. I wanted to be like Tom Brown. In fact, that evening after hearing him tell stories, I broke into the dark auditorium, walked up onto the stage, and stepped behind the lectern. I stood there staring out at 1,000 empty chairs, barely lit by the dim glow from a few exit signs. I thought to myself, "Someday, I'm going to speak to a full house like this." Little did I know where that conviction would take me.

I caught the "speaking bug." But I couldn't figure out how to make a living from just "talking to people," so I decided that I'd better get serious about getting a job. At that same time, my wife Angela and I decided we needed a change of pace. And so we left the mountains of Denver for the ocean in San Diego.

We showed up in San Diego in 1992 with no job, no friends, little money, broken-and-borrowed furniture and a crappy old Civic. Fortunately, I did land a job selling cell phones. That lasted about a year. Then I sold insurance for a few years. Then I finally discovered the recruiting industry, which suited me perfectly. Little did I know that it would literally change my life and lead me to Antarctica.

IN THE BUSINESS OF *FINDING* PEOPLE (RECRUITING)

I still remember my first day in the headhunting business back in 1997. A good friend of mine, Nathan Arnett, got me into the recruiting industry, working for a small recruitment company in Orange County, California. Although I drove 52 miles from La Jolla to Laguna Hills, braving the infamous Southern California freeways, it was worth it.

From day one, I fell in love with the recruiting business. I loved the conversations with hiring managers and leaders about what work needed to be done, what the profile of the ideal candidate was, and how we were going find the best people. To me it was more like a game than a "job."

During that time, I was on the road, criss-crossing the country by air, hitting dozens of cities every year. I loved this work. But I remember the bored looks from fellow airline passengers when I told them I was a recruiter guy. But then one day I stumbled into something fascinating. During one particularly successful trip I was jazzed, and when a fellow traveler asked me what I did for a living, I just blurted out, "I fly around the country, I party like a rock star, and I get to help companies find the best people in

America!" The guy stood there with his mouth hanging open, and he said, "I want a job like that!"

That little episode taught me the power of being different, and the importance of showcasing what you do in a succinct and compelling way. This draws people in, and leaves them wanting more.

A pretty good talent for a sales guy to have!

I also love the conversations I have with great candidates about who they are, what they love to do, and why they love to do it. The work of engaging in conversations like these rarely seemed like work to me, and it still doesn't. I have been actively involved in the recruiting (headhunting) business since that day in 1997.

NOW IN THE BUSINESS OF *KEEPING* PEOPLE (RETENTION)

Over the next few years I noticed a problem in corporate America. Many of my clients spent a lot of time and money *finding* great people—but when it came to *engaging* them, and *keeping* them, there was a huge drop off. I distinctly remember a conversation I had with one of my customers in 2001 when he looked at me and said, "Mike, this year we've hired 788 sales people, but we lost 802." I knew right away that I had broken into a different business—it wasn't just about *finding* people, it was about *keeping* them.

Over the years, many people have said to me, "Wow, it's *expensive* to hire people and use recruiting guys like you." My reply was, "Hey, if you think it's expensive to *hire* good people, try the cost of *losing* them! And worse yet, try calculating the cost of having someone on your team who isn't engaged… who doesn't really care…who's checked-out. That's *really* expensive!"

Studies conducted by companies such as the Gallup Organization have shown that only one out of five employees is fully engaged on a consistent basis. That's ONE-IN-FIVE! That's incredible. That's terrible. If your workplace were an eight-cylinder car, you'd be running on two cylinders every single day! If your car was misfiring that badly, your gas mileage would be cut in half. Would you put up with that? No! You'd take it to the shop for a tune-up, and if it couldn't be fixed, you'd replace it. It's easy to calculate reduction in auto performance, but it's hard to quantify reduction in *employee* performance. It's exactly the same concept, but in the business world it's much more expensive and far more important than taking care of a car.

Why do so many companies put up with this? I think the truth of the matter is that many of them have no idea this is happening. It's like a slow drip from your water faucet. It's easy to overlook. And your water bill keeps rising and rising.

Leading at 90 Below Zero is all about how to be more effective as a leader, so you can raise the probability that you and your team can find, engage and keep the very best performing people. The question for you is: "What are the factors within your control that will allow you to accomplish this?" As you go through the stories and principles in this book, take specific notes on how they can help you become a more effective leader.

So again, if you walk away from this book with one idea, one best practice, one specific actionable item that will allow you to become a better leader, you will have accomplished something worthwhile. If you take action and follow-through on that item, the results you and your team will achieve, will pay dividends for a long time.

DISCOVERY AT BARNES & NOBLE

Now, jumping to 2001, one night following a successful recruiting assignment, I found myself in Bakersfield, California. I was driving back to my hotel, and it occurred to me that I'd recently finished the book I'd been reading. Dang! As an avid reader, I always travel with one or two books. Just then I came upon a brightly lit Barnes & Noble bookstore. Do you believe in fate?

As usual, I headed straight for the Business section. Hey, I'm a practical kind of guy! I'm scanning the titles…*In Search of Excellence*—already read it. *See You at the Top*—already read it. *The Greatest Salesman in the World*—already read it (four times). Then I saw a book that had the most un-business-like cover I'd ever seen: It was a very old old black-and-white photo of a dozen men playing soccer… on an endless snowfield…and I thought to myself, "What is this?"

It was Ant-arc-tica!

The photo on the cover of Shackleton's Way

I looked more closely at the photo and noticed a wooden, four-masted sailing ship in the background. "What does this have to do with business?" I wondered.

The book's title was *Shackleton's Way*. I'd never heard of this guy Shackleton. And then I read the subtitle: "Leadership Lessons from the Great Antarctic Explorer."

I was intrigued. I didn't understand the connection between the picture on the cover, this guy Shackleton, and what any of it had to do with leadership and business. So I started thumbing through the book. I quickly discovered that this explorer had led 27 men to the bottom of the world, with the goal of doing something outrageous, something that no one had ever thought of, or dared to try. Ernest Shackleton's goal was to lead the first to cross the entire continent of Antarctica-on foot!

My instant thought was, "I wish I worked for a guy like this!" So I bought the book.

Back in my hotel room I didn't put that book down until 3am! (This was unprecedented, as I'm an early-morning kind of guy, I'm usually up by 5am!)

SOME GUY NAMED SHACKLETON

I was fascinated with Ernest Shackleton. The thought playing playing over and over in my mind was, "I wish I worked for a guy like Shackleton! I wish my team was more like his!"

Shackleton's goal was to make history. Little did he know that he *was* going to make history—but not for the reason he *expected*. You see, not only did Shackleton *not* cross Antarctica, his ship never got within 20 miles of the continent! Remember that photo of the guys playing soccer in front of that ship? That was Shackleton's ship stuck in the ice. The expedition he planned would go very differently than anyone expected.

Based on his ability to lead his men through difficult and dangerous situations, Ernest Shackleton is hailed as being one of the greatest leaders in the world! Don't take my word for it! This is what Sir Edmund Hillary—the first person to reach the summit of Mount Everest—said:

> "One heroic figure who impressed me very much indeed, and that was the great Antarctic explorer, Shackleton. Shackleton I always admired because he was a tough man and a very good

leader. And whenever he was in difficult circumstances, which he frequently was, he seemed to have the great ability to inspire his men and lead his party safely out of those conditions. So certainly Shackleton, I would have said, more than anything, was a role model for me.

And later on, when I was down in the Antarctic myself, I really felt that I tried to behave perhaps a little bit more like Shackleton, than any of the other famous Antarctic explorers."

And here's what Polar geologist Raymond Priestley had to say:

"For scientific leadership, give me Scott; for swift and efficient travel, Amundsen; but when you are in a hopeless situation, when there seems to be no way out, get on your knees and pray for Shackleton. Shackleton was a great leader because he balanced a vision, a plan, and maintained flexibility in how he was going to accomplish his goal in an ever-changing environment. This sounds to me like a great way to run our businesses!"

So anyway...It didn't take long for this Shackleton guy to become my hero and my role model, too! He was often quoted as saying things like, "I love it when things are hard and hate it when things are easy."

> *"I love it when thing are hard, and hate it when things are easy."*
>
> — ERNEST SHACKLETON

How great is *that?!* Shackleton wasn't one to take the easy way. He knew that the path to achievement and greatness is full of challenges—and he embraced those challenges! Transposing this into the real world, I thought, "This is how the best performing people think. They want challenge. They want to solve problems, not simply be handed the answers. They want to grow and use all their skills. They want to be fully employed, not underemployed. They think and act like Shackleton."

Now you can start to see why I was so drawn to Antarctica, and traveled there to run two marathons. It was not cold weather or sports, but rather the character of Shackleton as a leader that led me to the bottom of the world. After all, what kind of person would intentionally take a group of people to a destination that no one had ever been to or even thought about going to, especially if that destination was somewhere between difficult and dangerous.

Then it hit me: This is what the world's greatest companies do. They lead their people to places where nobody else in their industry has ever been. They're looking for ways to solve new problems and create better value for their customers; yes, this is between difficult and dangerous. This is why so few companies become excellent—and stay excellent. These are the companies that weathered the economic storms of 2008 better than others. In the end it all comes down to one thing: How well the leaders lead. And the question for you is: "What can you do to be more effective?"

> *"Great leaders take people to new destinations between difficult and dangerous."*
>
> — ANTARCTIC MIKE

Ernest Shackleton was one of the greatest leaders ever

I was impressed by the similarities between what it takes to be successful in Antarctica one-hundred years ago and the real world today. After all, the definition of an expedition is simple a journey with a specific purpose. Isn't that what we are trying to accomplish everyday? Shackleton's goal was to cross Antarctica on foot, some 1,800 miles! What's yours?

WHAT IS YOUR "ANTARCTICA"?

If you are ambitious, have dreams, a vision for your future, or specific goals, then you have your very own "Antarctica." Your Antarctica includes both your goals as well as the obstacles that stand in your way. As every ambitious person knows, if you're going to accomplish something great, there will be hazards along the way! Whether you're running a small business, a big business, or working for one, your goal is always to go from Point A to Point B.

There are obstacles and opportunities along the way, and those obstacles and opportunities often intersect. Very often, what initially looks like a straight line from Point A to Point B turns into a wildly zig-zagging path that takes you to C, D, E, F and G—before you finally get to B! The important question for you is this: Are you ready? Are you adequately prepared to conquer your own Antarctica and lead others across theirs?

CONNECTING ANTARCTICA TO BUSINESS

As I read more about Shackleton, I also began connecting the dots between his Antarctic adventures and our business efforts. I was drawn to Shackleton's character. He truly had the DNA of a great leader. You'll see that as the story unfolds.

I also began connecting the dots to building a professional speaking business I knew I had something unique here. I really wanted to tell stories from Antarctica, and share the many lessons that Shackleton has to teach us. The more I learned about this guy, the more excited I became. His life teaches us not only about leadership, but also about finding the right crew, and about keeping them engaged. And all of a sudden all of this connected with my career as an executive recruiter!

I was motivated to study about Shackleton more than I had ever been motivated to study about *anything* in college. In fact, I now own more books about Shackleton than I had read in all of my college courses combined!

But I still didn't see a way to integrate and implement all of my interests and experiences.

Then, a month after stumbling into *Shackleton's Way* in 2001, my boss asked me to teach a leadership class.

He handed me a "Leadership-Course-In-a-Box" program, pointed me out the door, and said, "Just teach what's written there!"

Well, I was thrilled to be finally be a speaker—but I didn't care for the mechanical, boring approach that the so-called "leadership experts" had compiled into four giant three-ring binders. Hey, you have to start somewhere! So I started traveling across the U.S. and Canada, teaching a course to VPs and managers called "Managing For Excellence." This was a top-rated business course written by John Kotter, a famous Harvard guy. It was a great course and made a lot of good points about how to lead more effectively. The problem was that it wasn't illustrated very well.

And that's when it clicked, literally. I was going to make the points of the program through stories and pictures from Shackleton's adventures—and make them my own. I was going to bring the life and lessons of Ernest Shackleton to the people in my audiences.

So I ran out to Barnes & Noble and I bought a big picture-book of Shackleton's "Imperial Trans-Antarctic Expedition." I cut out all the photos and matched them with different points in the leadership program that I was commissioned to teach. I figured that I would convey the basic content of the leadership program, but I would illustrate it my own way, with stories and illustrations of Shackleton's expedition.

I was a little nervous the first time I presented the program this way. Not because of the addition of Antarctica, but because I hadn't asked permission from any of my bosses. Well, my audiences *loved* hearing about Shackleton and Antarctica—but more importantly, they remembered the key points of the leadership program because they were linked to very compelling pictures and stories.

Well, from then on, the program got better and better, I had more and more fun, and my customers and their audiences learned more and more. I'll never forget one of the programs I taught in Indianapolis in 2002. At the end of the four-day leadership program, I went around the room asking each person to give a sentence or two that outlined their biggest takeaway from the leadership course. One guy said, "I don't even know where Antarctica is, but I'm fired up to go!" I knew at that point that he was totally engaged because of the stories and pictures. I also knew that his likelihood of actually remembering and using what he learned increased because of how engaged he was. I knew I had something really unique and special here. I loved my job. I could not believe I was getting paid to do this!

This was the beginning of a major turning point for me. I had combined two great ideas that led me down a path that wound across America, down to Antarctica and back again. The first great idea was *the power of a story.* The second great idea was that *people think in pictures, not in words.* This has forever changed the way I communicate.

Think back on all the schools, seminars and classes you've attended. What do you remember? If you're like most people, you remember a few of the powerful stories, including some of the key details. However, telling a story is not enough. You have to connect the points of a story to something that matters to the people in the audience. Then over time, as people remember the story, they also remember the point. This is why it's so important for leaders to be great story collectors and story tellers. That's why my entire work is based on a few powerful stories told in person with photos and videos.

Think about *your* story, and all the stories that lie under the roof of your company (stories about employees, customers, strategic partners and vendors). How well are you using those stories to attract and keep the very best people? The power of your stories will move people to want to do business with you. I'm speaking of both employees and customers. Your stories are *your* differentiator. How much of a difference are they making?

> *"People think in pictures, not in words."*
> —TOM ARNETT

FROM ONE COMPANY TO THOUSANDS

I loved my job working for SCI, and teaching "Managing For Excellence" and using the Antarctic stories to inspire people. I felt thankful, but very underemployed. One day I woke up and said, "I don't just want to do this for just *one* company. I want to do this for *hundreds* of organizations and *thousands* of people." How would I do this?

I discovered a group of people who are as crazy about speaking as I am. The National Speakers Association brings together people who speak professionally for a living. I was truly inspired, because I met kindred spirits, friends and mentors. One of the things I learned was that most speakers write books on their topics. It's a way to spread your message, and it lends credibility to the speaker.

Cool! I could write my own book on "Business Lessons Learned from Shackleton."

A speaker friend suggested that I should talk with a fellow speaker/author who had self-published a book, had sold two million copies, and had appeared on *Oprah*. I had to talk with this guy! The author was glad to chat with me because I was referred by a fellow speaker, and said he had about 15 minutes.

So I launched into my story: ". . . Blah-blah-blah Antarctica . . . Blah-blah-blah Shackleton . . . Blah-blah-blah leadership . . . Blah-blah-blah sales . . . Blah-blah-blah speaking."

"It sounds pretty good," he said, "Although conquering Antarctica isn't quite as inspiring as climbing Mount Everest. But it's still pretty exciting and rare. Yes, I agree that you've got a great shot at speaking on this, and writing a book about it." And then he asked, "So, what are your credentials for talking about Antarctica?"

"Well, I've read pretty much every book ever written about Antarctica and Ernest Shackleton!"

"But what's your *connection* to Antarctica?" he asked.

"What do you mean?"

"Well, was it your job or something else that caused you to visit Antarctica?"

"Um, I've never been to Antarctica."

There was a pause on the other end of the line. And then he exclaimed, "Well, hell! You can't *talk* about Antarctica unless you've *been* to Antarctica!"

"Why not?"

"Here's how it works. Audiences will pay to hear the experiences of a guy who has climbed Mount Everest. It's exciting! It's challenging! And the guy will be telling his own story!"

"But I can tell Shackleton's story!"

"Look, it's about credibility. Unless you've actually been there, you're missing an element of punch in the story. You've got to walk in the shoes of guys like Shackleton if you want to talk about them."

I was speechless.

He took pity on me and continued, "Is there any way you could get to Antarctica? Any reason for you to go?"

I paused, then remembered something. "Well, the first-ever Antarctic Ice marathon is being held next year and—"

"That's *it!!* You're *in!!*" he cried. "If you run a marathon in Antarctica, then people will pay attention to you!" He then added, "Um, have you ever run a marathon?"

"I ran one back in college. But that was 20 years ago."

"Hey, the more you struggle, the more you're walking in the shoes of the guys who were there a hundred years ago. Look, you don't have to *win* the marathon!

Just *participating* will give you an outrageous experience that lots of people would love to hear about!"

"You're right, Greg. I'm signing up for the marathon in Antarctica." And I hung the phone up and sat there in the car, still a bit dazed from that conversation.

It was February of 2005 and I had spent over an hour on the phone with a guy I couldn't even have picked out of a police lineup to save my life. It was pouring down rain, as I sat in my Volvo in the Starbucks parking lot on Clairemont Mesa Boulevard off the 805.

The first ever Antarctic Ice Marathon, January 5, 2006

I was thrilled. I knew I could get in marathon-shape in six months. What I wasn't so sure about . . . was convincing Angela that I should fly 12,000 miles, at a cost of nearly $20,000, to run 26.2 miles.

And so, later that day, back at home . . . I spilled the beans to my wife Angela.

"Where?!"

"Antarctica."

"To do *what??*"

"Run a marathon."

"When's the last time you ran a marathon?"

"Back in college."

"And *why* do you want to do this crazy stunt?"

"To walk in the shoes of Shackleton."

"Who gave you this brilliant idea?"

"This guy named Greg Godek."

"Greg *who?* How do you know him?"

"Well, I just met him over the phone, but he's right. If I'm going to speak about Shackleton and the guys who first put Antarctica on the map, I have to follow in their footsteps!"

"Well, okay then."

And that was that.

Have I mentioned that I have The Best Wife in the Whole Wide World?

Eleven months later, on Friday, January 5th, 2006, I was one of nine runners from five countries to take part in the first ever Antarctic Ice Marathon. Yes, that's a full marathon—26.2 miles—run on an ice shelf in the middle of nowhere, just 600 miles from the South Pole. How I trained and prepared for this is *another* story...one I'll get to soon. It was crazy, challenging and life-changing. And in hindsight, it was one of the most powerful learning experiences I've ever had. It affected me deeply, and I learned a lot about life and about business.

Why did I do this? It wasn't to prove something. It wasn't for the publicity. It was because I needed to walk—or run—in Shackleton's shoes. I needed to get a taste of what he and his crew went through—physically, mentally and emotionally—in order to tell their story with conviction, confidence and certainty.

My experiences in Antarctica changed my life in ways that I wasn't expecting. You'll see how that ties into my story soon. But back to the subject of Antarctica.

Let me give you a few facts about this place so you'll understand the context of Shackleton's story. You see, this program isn't for Antarctic history buffs, or for cold-weather fans, or for athletes. This program is for *you*. For people who want to lead, who want to succeed, who want to strive and to conquer. These Antarctic stories drive home the importance of concepts like personal goals, perseverance, teamwork and leadership. These are important concepts here in the real world of business.

> *"Better to aim high and miss the target than to aim low and hit it."*
>
> — LES BROWN

A FEW ANTARCTIC FACTS

The continent of Antarctica is more than 500 million years old. It used to be connected to several other land masses including Australia and India. Around 20 million years ago it broke apart from the other land masses and it slowly drifted southward where it sits today, at the bottom of the world. And so for the last 20 million years it's been doing nothing other than sitting there collecting ice and snow. As a matter of fact, within the Antarctic Circle, which is the 66.5 degree latitude mark, is two-thirds of all the fresh water in the world—and 90 percent of all the ice on the planet.

5.5 million square miles of ice and snow

The continent of Antarctica covers 5.5 million square miles. That's about the size of the United States and Mexico. And that entire landmass is covered by ice that averages one mile thick! And at the South Pole the ice is more than *two* miles thick! And that's why the elevation of the South Pole is 10,000 feet. That's nearly twice the elevation of the mile-high city of Denver!

The ice that covers Antarctica is so heavy that it actually submerges the land mass more than half a mile into the depths of the Southern Ocean! If you stripped the ice off Antarctica, the island continent would rise up out of the sea by more than half a mile. It's mind-boggling!

Now, even though Antarctica is 500 million years old, and the human race is about 200,000 years old, it wasn't until nearly 200 years ago that any human got remotely close to Antarctica! Why? Because the worst weather in the world and the roughest ocean on earth surround this ice-bound continent. In the late 1700's whaling ships from Spain and Portugal first ventured into the region. It was the profit motive that first caused people to push close to Antarctica. Whales were the target because their oil was a valuable commodity.

I think it's fascinating that the business people led the way, not the explorers or scientists! It was curiosity and the urge to explore that finally motivated people to actually step foot onto Antarctica, which first occurred nearly 100 years later in 1821. And then, of course—people being people—the urge to explore became a contest to be the first to reach the South Pole!

I mentioned earlier that the Antarctic is full of challenges and elements and enemies. What you see here is one of those enemies. It's called the Katabatic Winds.

The Katabatic winds are one of the biggest challenges in the Antarctic

These are gravity-driven winds that pick up speed as they race downhill, reaching hurricane speeds of 100-mph or more. To add to the challenge, these winds carry a lot of ice and snow. After all, we're in Antarctica!

Here in the business world we face challenges and enemies, too. Sometimes they're predictable, and sometimes not. Sometimes our challenges come one at a time, and sometimes the wind and the snow and the ice and the cold all gather together into a hurricane-like set of challenges! Competition, changing customer demands, an every-changing economy, and many other elements—all of which are largely out of your control, and mostly unpredictable.

Oh, and then there are the crevasses! These cracks in the ice—often hundreds of feet deep—sometimes hide in plain sight among the white snow and ice, and sometimes hide under a thin layer of ice and snow. On my second of two trips to Antarctica I had lunch with a guy who had once fallen into a crevasse. He had hung upside down for eight hours during a winter storm. It was minus 42 degrees Farhenheit. (And that's *without* a wind chill factor!) His hand had turned solid black and would have to be amputated when he returned home.

Yes, crevasses in Antarctica are a very real danger. And metaphorically speaking, they're also found in the real world. It's called change. In your career have you ever stepped onto a surface that you thought was solid, and suddenly found yourself falling? Things can change in an instant. Whether you were in Antarctica 100 years ago, or in the real world today. Sudden and unexpected change is a part of everyday life. But great leaders are always prepared.

Sudden and unexpected change is something we all have to be prepared for everyday

Your business challenges are similar to those faced by the Antarctic explorers. We all have challenges and enemies—and these elements are never going to go away. So whether you're going on an Antarctic adventure, or pursuing a business adventure, or tackling any other responsibility that you consider important, you need to prepare—and you you need to manage the factors that are within your control. In this way, you can move forward despite the presence of those challenges and enemies. Great leaders understand how to manage the enemies and elements.

Many of these "enemies and elements" are the reason that so few people today are fully engaged in what they do for a living. Leaders have a responsibility to help people manage the "enemies and elements" that can so easily make the journey difficult and dangerous. I'll dive into the specifics of what specific enemies cause people to be more or less engaged as the story unfolds.

THE CONQUEST FOR THE SOUTH POLE BEGINS

One of the first serious attempts to reach the South Pole occurred in 1902. This was a British expedition led by Robert Scott, a captain in the Royal Navy. Shackleton was the third officer on this expedition. After sailing 12,000 miles from England to the edge of Antarctica, they wintered over at the continent's edge.

The next spring, they began their march to the South Pole, a distance of nearly 800 miles. They had traveled 200 miles inland when Scott made the decision to turn back because of harsh weather conditions. He fell short of his goal by nearly 600 miles. So on the one hand we can say that Scott's expedition failed—because they didn't reach the South Pole. On the other hand we can say they were successful—because they pushed 200 miles further into the frozen continent than anyone had ever done before.

The Discovery Expedtion of 1902

Upon their return to England, Scott and Shackleton parted ways. Different leadership philosophies had caused serious friction between the two of them. Scott was a "by the book" kind of guy: He followed the long tradition of keeping the officers and the crew well separated from each other.

In the British naval world, officers and crew dressed differently, they ate and slept separately, and the division of labor was specific and absolute. Thus, aboard ship there were two groups of men: The haves and the have-nots.

Shackleton was ahead of his time in believing that everyone on the ship should be respected, treated well, and befriended. He bucked the strict class system of British society and the traditions of the seafaring life.

Shackleton's observation during his expedition with Scott was that this class system wasn't as effective as it could be—and in fact, it could be downright danger-ous. He knew that everyone held different roles and different responsibilities, and that each person was accountable for specific activities. But he also believed that a ship should be run as an integrated team, and that everyone deserved to be treated equally. He saw that—in difficult and life-threatening situations—a strict division of labor could inhibit decision-making, damage morale, and decrease performance.

But of course, Shackleton was merely the third officer on that first expection. And Scott, as the leader of the team—or metaphorically, the owner of the business—decided that his "employee" Shackleton wasn't the right man for the job anymore. So they parted ways.

Shackleton gave up reaching the South Pole for the wellbeing of his crew

In October of 1908 Shackleton and three companions started their southern trek toward the South Pole. They set a record for reaching the farthest south latitude to date (88 degrees, 23 minutes South). Then with only 97 miles to go, Shackleton made a very difficult and important decision to abort the mission and turn back for home.

His teammates cried, "Are you out of your mind? We're less than 100 miles from being the first human beings to reach the bottom of the world! Let's keep going!" (Well, I'm sure they said something similar to that.) Why would Shackleton travel nearly 13,000 miles, spend three years of his life, and put his reputation on the line—only to turn around and head home?

Why? One simple reason: Shackleton felt that the margin of safety was too thin and that they would likely run out of supplies. This was a very agonizing decision for Shackleton. On the one hand, he was just 97-miles from greatness. Think about the fame, the fortune, the sense of accomplishment, and his place in history. On the other hand, he was only 97-miles from possible disaster, if they had run out of supplies. What does the fact that he turned around despite being so close to his goal, tell you about his character as a leader? What lesson is the lesson for you in this situation?

Shackleton valued the well-being of his men more than he valued fame and fortune. He didn't allow the emotion, the euphoria, or being a mere 97-miles from his goal blind him to the reality of the moment. Sure, they could have made it to the South Pole, but would they have enough supplies to get them back? Don't forget that once they reached their goal, they would have to turn around and trek another 800 miles back to their ship. When they got to the bottom of the world it was not like they could be picked-up by a plane.

You see, Shackleton was more concerned about the well-being of his men than he was about the goal. They meant more to him than the glory, the honor, or the money, that awaited him by being the first person to reach the South Pole.

Would you call Shackleton a failure? I am convinced he's not only a success—he's a role model for what a great leader should be. Shackleton could make objective decisions in the middle of chaotic situations. He was committed to the goal, yet flexible enough to change the course of action when it was necessary. He could make the hard decisions that people didn't necessarily like, but would eventually save their lives. The bottom line is that he put the needs of his team ahead of what *he* wanted and needed.

That's a *real* leader, folks; somebody you'd want to follow, so willingly and enthusiastically. People will want to follow a leader who puts their interests ahead of what their leader wants. This is a key to leading and engaging people effectively.

I don't think you could ever find a person more enthusiastic and visionary than Ernest Shackleton. And yet he also was that rare person who was grounded firmly in reality. Shackleton refused to give in to what we now call "summit fever." Summit fever takes over when people believe, "I must get to the top at all costs." While continuing to plunge forward, they disregard safety, reality, ethics and just plain common sense. Summit fever is a common affliction of Mount Everest climbers.

The bestseller *Into Thin Air* recounts the story of a 1996 Mount Everest climb led by Scott Fischer in which the team did make the summit—but many of them, including Fischer, perished on the descent. This was one of the most tragic mountaineering disasters in recorded history. Summit fever had doomed them. Summit fever overtakes people when they allow ego, or ambition, or peer pressure, or greed, or a "win-at-all-costs" mindset to impede their good judgment, and prevents them from making sound decisions.

Ernest Shackleton was a driven man. He had outrageous goals, and he certainly had an ego bigger than most; big enough to take him where few people would dare to go. Heck, anyone who would lead an expedition to the bottom of the world—or to the top of Mount Everest—is one confident son-of-a-gun!

Great leaders of companies have pretty darn big egos too! You simply can't achieve greatness with average-sized goals and average-sized egos! The problem is not with egos, but with egos that aren't managed and kept under control. I find it interesting that the word "ego" gets a bad rap. It's like people's knee-jerk reaction to the word "steroids." When I said that word just now, I'll bet that many of you instantly thought, "Abuse," or "Illegally pumped-up athlete." But steroids—when properly used—save people's lives! Likewise, egos—when properly used—can lead to outrageous success and accomplishment. But the important question is, "Who's in control here, you or your ego?"

Shackleton had a big ego, but a healthy one. (After all, an uncertain, insecure person does not set huge, visionary, historic goals.) He held his ego in check. His intellect ruled his emotions, and he continued to see his situation through an objective lens. He put the safety of his men—and the overall success—the long-term success—of his mission, ahead of any short-term or emotional considerations. For this reason, even though he was within a hundred miles of his goal, he turned his team around and headed for home. He demonstrated what a great leader should do.

> *"I'm actually as proud of the things we haven't done as the things I have done. Innovation is saying no to 1,000 things."*
>
> —STEVE JOBS

As a leader in your organization, put yourself in Shackleton's shoes. You've worked hard toward a goal or accomplishment that you want. You've risked a lot to get to where you are. Ask yourself this important question: Are your goals in alignment, or in conflict with respect to what's best for the team? I'm not saying you can't have dreams and go for what you want. What I am saying is that if your goals and dreams are not in the best interest of the team you lead, you need to ask yourself some really honest questions that are not easy to answer.

I got an interesting phone call about two years ago from a business owner in Calgary, Alberta. He had heard me speak at a CEO roundtable group a few months prior to calling me.

He told me a story of his own that related to Shackleton's decision to turn back just 97 miles from the South Pole.

"Mike, I thought long and hard about that Shackleton story for *days* after the meeting. Three years ago, my company made a decision that we were going to expand our business by going into Indonesia. After thinking about Shackleton and how he put his men first, I went back to my board and we discussed whether or not going into Asia was really in the best interest of everybody in the company—not just me. After about a week of agonizing discussions and analyses, we came to the conclusion that it was not in the best interest of the company to enter the Asian market at that time."

"Your story about Shackleton turning back gave me the confidence to be flexible enough to change my mind. It was too much about me and not enough about my team. I appreciate the lessons that you and Shackleton have brought to my company."

Every day leaders have to think objectively about what's really in the best interest of the team, collectively. Human nature tells us to grab what's ours and what we've worked hard for. Great leaders remain objective and put the interest of their people first, even in those moments when the degree of emotional charge is high. Quite frankly, anyone can make those decisions when the risk factors are low and level of emotional charge is minimal. Up the ante, and this separates a *real* leader from someone who merely *looks* like a leader.

I was on a plane traveling to a speaking engagement about six months ago. There was an older gentleman sitting next to me. We got into a conversation about what I did for a living and what he did before he retired, years ago. Turned out he was a former sales rep for Bell South, selling PBX systems and long distance services to companies.

We were talking about the part of the story where Shackleton turned around with 97-miles to South Pole in order to save the lives of his men. We were discussing how heard it is to focus on other people when there is so much on the line for you personally. My seatmate proceeded to tell me a story that I'll never forget that illustrates this point.

This gentleman then told me a story that I'll never forget.

"In 1971, I had a million dollar quota working for Bell South. I was on a sales call with a prospective customer who wanted to hire us to do a $300,000 job. That's a big deal, as it was 30 percent of my annual quota!"

"The customer said, 'We want you to do A, B, and C, and we'd like it done in this timeframe. I'm ready to sign a check and contract today.'"

"I looked at him and said, 'Thank you for your confidence in me, but before I say yes, let me make sure we can actually deliver *what* you want, *when* you want it.'"

"So I went back to my engineering and project management people. I returned to my customer and said, 'We *can* do A, B and C. However, we *can't* do it in your timeframe. However, I can *still* help you. I've already called one of my competitors and explained the situation. They can do A, B, and C, *and* they can meet your deadline. He's expecting your call.' So my customer called my competitor and the deal was done."

This is a very difficult thing for a sales person to do. So many sales training courses and business books teach us to grab the check and contract and get out before the client changes his or her mind. It would be so tempting to take the business and try and jam it into what the customer wants, when they want it. It takes a very other-centered person to say "No," like my seatmate did.

He continued his story:

> "Six months later I get a call from that same client. This time he requests X, Y and Z, but then he added, 'Regarding the timeframe, we'll work within *your* timeframe this time. We're going with Bell South because you proved to us that you truly put *our* needs ahead of *yours.*'"

> "Needless to say, I was pleased. But when he told me that it was a $900,000 order I was speechless!"

> *"What would you attempt to do if you knew you could not fail?"*
>
> —ROBERT SCHULLER

This is a great story that demonstrates what can happen when you really do put the needs of others ahead of what you want and need. Great leaders do this consistently. They see what they need and want as a by-product, not as their focus. The focus is on the other person or the team. Shackleton demonstrated this time and time again.

RACE TO THE SOUTH POLE

Ernest Shackleton's goal had been to be the first person to reach the South Pole. He and his team fell just 97 miles short of that goal, although the decisions he made as a leader saved their lives.

Back in England Shackleton began planning a new Polar expedition. But before he could regroup, two other guys mounted their own expeditions with the goal of reaching the South Pole. A British team and a Norwegian team headed south within days of one another.

The Norwegian team was led by Roald Amundsen, a hearty fellow who was also the first person to navigate the Northwest Passage, the body of water connecting the Pacific and Atlantic Oceans through Canada. For hundreds of years, many ships and men had disappeared in the quest to find this passage.

*The race to the South Pole between England's Robert Scott (L),
and Norway's Roald Amundsen (R)*

The British team was led by Robert Scott. Remember him? He was the guy who parted ways with Shackleton from that earlier expedition! Well, both Amundsen and Scott reached the South Pole. But their trips were vastly—and tragically—different.

The Norwegians won the race, and became the first people to step foot at the South Pole on December 14, 1911. The Brits arrived just a few weeks later in January, 1912. But let's not forget that *reaching* the South Pole is only half the challenge. The other half is *returnig home* to tell the story.

Well, this is where the story gets interesting, and has a number of real world lessons for all of us. These include preparation, discipline and consistency of activity.

The Norwegians implemented *their* plan like clock-work. In fact, Amundsen's trek from his base camp to the South Pole, and back again—a trip of approximately 1,600 miles—took 99 days, which was within a few days of what his plan called for. When you think of the thousands of variables involved, it's a truly astounding feat! What accounted for Amundsen's success? Preparation, discipline and consistency of activity. Part of their preparation was a complete analysis of the provisions required for the round-trip. Another part of their plan was to march 6 hours a day, covering about 15-20 miles/day. Period. Consistency of effort was more important than any one day's progress.

Now, sadly, over on the British side, their preparations were inconsistent, and they changed their plan midstream. Although Scott and his team did reach the South Pole, they all perished on their return trip—just 10 miles from a depot box (supply box with food and fuel) they had set for themselves on the way down. Why? Well, let's see. First of all, their progress was incredibly inconsistent.

Their daily mileage was all over the map. Some days it was 40 miles, and other days it was two.

There were many other differences in the way these teams were put together, planned, and run. For example: On Amundsen's team three of the four men were trained navigators. This greatly increased their chances of staying on course. On Scott's team only one of the five was a trained navigator.

Another example is the manner in which each team marked their supply depots so they could be found in a raging blizzarad. Scott's team simply placed one pennant on each depot box. This meant that as they trekked hundreds of miles they had to hit the bullseye or miss the target altogther. Amundsen's team set a *series* of flags, stretching three miles to each side of each depot box. In addition, each flag was marked with a directional arrow pointing toward the depot.

In the end, what it really came down to is that Amundsen and his men were more adequately prepared. They were more disciplined, and they stuck to the plan. Amundsen's approach was more proactive. Meanwhile, the British were not nearly as prepared, and they operated in a more reactive fashion than the Norwegians.

Great leaders and top performers in every area of business know that consistency of effort is one of the keys to success. The salesperson who makes 10 calls per day—five days a week, week-after-week—will be more successful than the salesperson who rushes through 50 calls in one day, then slacks off for the rest of the week. Both salespeople make 50 calls per week, but the 10-calls-per-day guy is going to be more successful. It's been proven time and time again.

In addition to consistency of effort, sticking to the plan is important, too. The second big mistake the British made was changing their plan at the last minute. Scott's plan was to support *four* people, including himself, to the pole. Scott decided to add a *fifth* member to the team. Scott's decision to add someone else wasn't the mistake. Rather, the mistake was failing to adjust their plan to compensate for extra food and supplies needed for another person. Unbelievably, the Brits didn't adjust their food supplies, or equipment, or number of sled dogs. This doomed them to failure. On the return journey, all five members of that British party died from starvation, three of them just 10 miles from one of the depot boxes.

There were many other differences in how they organized and led their teams. It's a fascinating story of two leaders, comparing the right way to lead and the wrong way to lead. (This will the topic of an upcoming book and program!)

The big difference between the Norwegian and the British really came down to one most important thing—discipline. In fact, the business book *Great By Choice*, by Jim Collins, uses the story of the Amundsen-Scott race to the South Pole as a metaphor to illustrate the importance of discipline. His contention is that discipline is not just what you *do*—it's also what you *don't* do. For example, it took

discipline for Amundsen to consisten[...]
20 miles every day. But it also took discip[...]
to *not* travel any farther than that!

> *"Discipline is not just what you do,*
> *but what you* don't *do."*
>
> — JIM COLLINS

For example, it took extraordinary discipline for Amundsen's team to travel 15 to 20 miles in a blinding snowstorm while the British stopped and spent the day in their tents, making no progress whatsoever. Conversely, on a day when the weather was favorable, and the British traveled 30 or 40 miles, the Norwegians had the discipline to travel 15 to 20 miles...and no further.

The simplistic strategy of "faster-faster, harder-harder" doesn't always work. Common sense is just as important as passion and strength. Even race car drivers use their brakes! Both the Norwegians and the British achieved their goal of reaching the South Pole. In a way, they both "won." However, only the Norwegian team came back alive. Maybe it's just me, but the "Winning-at-all-costs" strategy seems kinda stupid. I mean, living through the experience seems rather important to me!

dy travel 15 to
ine for him

ot just what you
s all about balance.
ader, and you look
im, how do you see
you and your team
d is good. But push-
ut a break, without
evaluate what you're
doing, witho..   e—will lead to short-term success but long-term burnout. Metaphorically speaking, the best way to burn out the engine of your employee is to drive them fast and furiously, instead of skillfully and consistently. Consistency of effort is crucial to the long-term success of any team.

Okay, back to Shackleton…

> *"Sometimes the fastest way to the goal is to slow down."*
>
> **— ANTARCTIC MIKE**

"THE LAST GREAT JOURNEY ON EARTH"

Remember, Shackleton's goal had been to be the first person to reach the South Pole. Now that two teams have beaten him to his goal, what does he do? He comes up with an even *more* outrageous plan, one that shocked even the heartiest of the hearty. Soon after the South Pole was reached by Amundsen and Scott, Shackleton set a new goal: To lead the first team of people on a journey not only *to* the Pole, but all the way through it *to the other side of the continent*, a distance of nearly 1,800 miles! Their goal was a trans-continental crossing of Antarctica! Nobody else in history had ever done this or considered doing so. It would re-write the Polar history books. If you were in Vegas, this would be like going all in, as it was a big gamble on Shackleton's part. One of Shackleton's great leadership characteristics was that he *created* history instead of reading about others' accomplishments.

He was all about doing things that nobody had ever thought of, or dared to attempt.

Likewise, leaders today who take their companies to places where no competitor has ever gone, is what attracts and keeps the best people. I can tell you from my 20+ years in the recruiting business that the very best people are attracted to companies who are on the forefront of their industry and who have a vision to accomplish things that no other company has tried or considered. They want to be part of an organization that is achieving new things, solving problems in ways that nobody has thought of, and adding value in ways that customers have not yet experienced. They want to follow a leader like Shackleton. Are you that leader? Is your company pushing forward to create history in your industry?

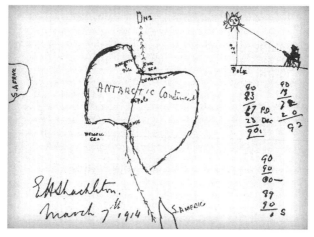

Shackleton's plan for "The Last Great Journey on Earth"—written on a napkin!

This picture is Shackleton's plan to cross the continent. He drew this image on a napkin at a fundraising dinner! This was his business plan! Can you imagine drafting your business plan on a napkin for the VC's and private equity guys? Shackleton's plan was a bold attempt to write the next chapter in Polar history. It was a daring plan to do what nobody else had ever attempted or considered. That's bold leadership!

When you create more value, solve more problems and help your customers create more differentiation in their marketplace, it changes the dynamic of the relationship in many ways. You're now perceived as a partner, not just a vendor.

Suddenly, price is not nearly as important. Now you've just separated yourself head-and-shoulders above your competitors. Companies that do this will attract and keep better people. This, in turn, helps you to survive the elements, and stand the test of time.

> *"Great companies are led by people who* create *history in their industry, instead of riding on the coattails of others."*
>
> — ANTARCTIC MIKE

In your business or industry, is there something that no other person or company has ever attempted before? Are there problems that your customers are experiencing that nobody in your industry has discovered or addressed? What value has nobody ever brought to the table of customers in your space? It may not require reinventing the wheel, but rather, tweaking the one that already exists. People who live and work in this fashion are the ones who make an impact and a difference, not just a living. This is what top performing people, both employees and customers, want from a top performing organization.

SHOWCASING THE OPPORTUNITY

With his plan in mind, Shackleton now sets out to showcase his opportunity. In order to pull off such a feat, he needs the very best people for the job, so he runs this ad. Read through it carefully. What strikes you? This ad was wildly successful, attracting more than 5,000 responses! Yes, that's correct, more than 5,000! Why do you think Shackleton's ad worked so well?

Shackleton's ad for recruiting crew members for the Endurance Expedition

The magic was in how he showcased this expedition. Just look at the headline. "MEN WANTED." Right away it grabs you and pulls you in. What else about this ad jumps at you? Is it the transparency and honesty of what this job really was? (not hiding the dangers). Is it the honor and recognition? Is it the challenge and difficulty of doing something you've never done before? Is it the sense of adventure? Whether you're in the Antarctic in 1914 or here in the business world in the 21st century, people want to work in a setting that's advendurous, where there are challenges, and they want to be led by someone who can successfully lead them.

How do you showcase *your* opportunity? Does it scream with adventure? Is it challenging enought to get the very best people to want to be a part of your company? Or, does it blend in with all the others and get lost in the *sea of similarity*?

Shackleton's ad is a key to unlocking the door and enabling us to showcase who we are, what we do, and why we do it in a way that stands out, attracts top performing people, and compels them to take action.

Here is a copy of an ad I wrote for a customer who is in the funeral and cemetery business. You can imagine how difficult it is for them to attract people to their industry. Well, I used that to our advantage, by coming out and saying just, exactly that. What do you notice in this ad? How is this different than most of the ads you see?

Service Corporation International

US-IL-Bloomington/Peoria-IMPERIAL TRANS-ILLINOIS SALES EXPEDITION

Ernest Shackleton in the early 1900's changed the course of Polar history and the lives of many people forever when he launched his "Endurance" expedition to the South Pole.

We, like Shackleton, are navigating a course that few organizations have traveled. We are seeking sales warriors who have achieved significant results in the past and want to take their accomplishments even higher. If you have drive and ambition like very few, are willing to be stretched and challenged beyond what you have ever experienced, have a great attitude and a teachable spirit, and want to reap rewards that many wish for but few attain, then respond to this ad. We are not looking for those seeking just employment, but wish to be part of an challenging expedition.

SCI is positioned to have the same impact on the lives of many people in Illinois with the launch of Dignity Memorial. We offer a stellar compensation plan complete with 401k, medical/dental/vision, stock bonus plan, bonuses, and more. We are the world's largest organization in the cemetery and funeral service industry. We are traded on the NYSE under the symbol SRV and can be seen at www.sci-corp.com.

We fully realize that this opportunity is not for everyone. Of course this is a subject that nobody wants to discuss, but one that everyone needs. Think about all the baby boomers over the next 20-30 years who will be our customer. Someone is going to get the business. Why not you? Don't think too long or the position will be filled. Along with your reply, send a 3-4 sentence write up on your most significant career accomplishment. We will read every response and will get back with you and give you an opportunity to advance to the next level.

SCI is an equal opportunity employer M/F/D/V

Additional Information
Position Type: Full Time, Part Time, Employee

Contact Information
Mark Bruce
mark.bruce@sci-us.com
Service Corporation International

Click here to see all "Service Corporation International" opportunities

APPLY ONLINE

Is your opportunity showcased in a way that grabs the attention of the best people?

WHAT WOULD SHACKLETON DO?...

. . . if he were in charge of showcasing *your* opportunity? Let's assume he was alive and well in 2015, and in his prime. If he were a key member of your team and was responsible responsible for finding, engaging and keeping the very best people, how would he showcase your company's oppoutunity?

If he had all the advantages of the internet, YouTube, Facebook and LinkedIn, what would he do? How would he tell the story? How would he broadcast it to the right audience? How would he make it stand out from the competition, get noticed and get a great response? How would he use the other members of your team to get their help and input?

One thing I know for sure is that Shackleton would use video to tell your story and the stories of your employees, customers, vendors, partners and others associated with your company. The collective power of your stories is what can make the difference. A hundred years ago, there was no internet, no videos used to tell stories for recruiting purposes, and no social media. Shackleton today would go to your people, employees, customers, and others connected with your company and he would uncover the stories—stories that tell why your people have chosen to work at your company and why they stay, stories from customers who buy from you, many of whom drive further and pay more for your products or services than what your competitors offer.

Why is this important? Those stories are what create the leverage to recruit great people and land great customers. Those stories are what separates you from your competitors. The stories should not only tell the audience *what* you do, *how* you do it, but *why* you do it. If you can uncover the WHY behind the faces of your employees, customers, vendors and partners associated with your organization, then you've created a strong point of differentiation and powerful magnet that draws in the best people.

Coming up with specific ideas for this is a great opportunity to get your co-workers involved. Hold a contest. Ask your customers for help. Put it out on social media and offer a prize for the winning selection. This is how the Nashville Predators (NHL) came up with a very different way to showcase their opportunity by creating a unique tagline. Sean Henry, the President of the team and a good friend of mine, put it out to their fan base on Twitter. One of the Nashville fans came up with "Smashville." The prize? A season ticket for life. Wow!

You will be amazed at how many great ideas are right in front of you. What is important is tapping into pool of people associated with your organization-employees, customers, vendors, partners. Remember this: *People support a world that they help create.* If you get your people involved, not only will you likely come up with some great ideas, you'll get them much more engaged and anchored to you. When they have some of their own skin in the game, the game changes.

> *"People will support a world they help create."*
>
> — TOM ARNETT

Imagine all the stories that you might uncover. Consider holding a contest among your employees (and maybe including customers). Create several teams and assign specific tasks to capture stories.

One team's task might be to capture the best reasons for working for your company. Their goal should be to create a 60-second "commercial" or YouTube piece.

Maybe another team's task is to discover why customers drive further and pay more for your product or service. They might also be able to help you create a 60-second "commercial" or YouTube piece. Customer stories are invaluable and one of the strongest marketing moves a company can make.

Another team's task is to explore how your company provides the very best products or services in your industry. Same goal: A 60-second piece.

This exercise will do two important things. First, it will generate a lot of creative, effective and imple-mentable ideas. And second, it will engage everyone who participates. Why is that important? Beause *people will help support a world that they help create.*

THE CALL TO ACTION

When using stories for recruiting purposes, I highly recommend ending with a *call to action*. This can manifest itself in many ways. You can ask a question, make a request, or offer a suggestion. Personally, I like asking a question—one that's intriguing and different. Remember, the goal here is not to sell your company or ask for a big commitment. You're simply encouraging someone to take another step.

For example, you might say something like this: "Does this sound like something you'd like to know more about? If so, please send us a write up of your most significant accomplishment, outlining what you did, how you did it, and what the measured results were."

Here's another good idea, from a company in Ontario, California, for recruiting sales people. "If you'd like to know more about this, please call 800-555-5555 and leave a 60-second message telling us why you have an interest and why you should be considered a serious candidate. Please be specific, but don't leave a message longer than 60 seconds." This is a great idea, as it requires candidates to take a step beyond sending an email, which anyone can do. It also gives the company a great opportunity to hear what someone actually sounds like on the phone. It also forces the candidate to be concise.

CHOOSING THE RIGHT PEOPLE FOR THE JOB

Back to Shackleton…With more than 5,000 responses to his ahis recruitment ad, he narrows the pool down to 1,000, then 100, and finally to the final 27 men he felt were the best for the job. If there's one word I'd use to label his selection criteria, it would be *character*. Of course Shackleton evaluated each candidate's skills and experience. But those were just the initial filters. His final decisions were based on each man's character.

In order to hire the right person for a particular job, one of the most important things to consider is their character. How are they wired? What are their inborn talents and aptitudes—what I call "Business DNA."

You need to get down to the "real" person. This is more important than the surface facts of pedigree, college degree and previous experience. We all know that resumes are subject to "enhancement." No resume can capture the all-important "real" person.

As a recruiting guy with more than 20 years in the employee selection business, I can tell you that most resumes are not worth the paper they're printed on. They do a terrible job of helping hiring managers understand the person from an objective perspective.

Besides, most candidates "embellish" their resumes beyond belief. Wouldn't you agree?

In order to discover the "real" person, one needs the right assessment tool. In addition, the correct understanding and application of what the assessment tells you is really important. There are a lot of assessments that give you data, numbers, charts and colors. What do the results *mean*—specifically, practically, and expressed in plain English—what I call "First Grade English." What do you *do* with all this information? How do you apply it?

Data and measurements are important, but interpreting them is even more important. (If you'd like any help with this, give me call! I can put you in touch with the people and companies in the assessment business who can best help you.)

Shackleton didn't have the benefit of modern psychological personality assessments, but he certainly understood the importance of understanding the character of the men he interviewed before selecting the ones for the job.

Asking great questions that get at key moments in people's lives and careers is also an important part of the assessment process. Personally, I am a strong proponent of uncovering what people have done that shows they are disciplined, focused and can work hard.

I also want to look back to their earliest years—even when they were a kid—because this shows how much discipline they had during their most formidable years.

When I explore this with a prospective candidate I bring up how I had a morning newspaper route as a 12 year old kid. I woke up in the dark seven days a week at 4:15am to schlep newspapers through the rain, snow and anything else that Allentown, PA threw at me. I did this for years. One thing I learned was that the work day begins at 4:30am. To this day, some 40 years later, I still wake up around 4am every single day. I attribute a lot of my discipline to my newspaper route. *This* is the kind of thing I want to know about someone I'm assessing.

ANTARCTICA BOUND!

Ok, now that Shackleton has his crew of 27 hand-selected men, it's time to go. He had planned on leaving England on August 5, 1914. This was the dawn of WW1, the same day that Winston Churchill called for a naval mobilization in preparation for the looming war. Delaying his departure, Shackleton sent a telegram to Winston Churchill volunteering himself, his ship and his crew to fight for England. Churchill answered Shackleton with a one-word telegram: "Proceed."

This is another example of Shackleton demonstrating what it means to be a great leader. He put the needs of England ahead of his expedition. Think about how hard that must have been. He had been planning and dreaming of this journey for years. He risked everything to launch it. Yet on the dawn of leaving he was willing to give it all up to fight for England. (Which was not even his homeland! Shackleton was Irish.)

Putting other people ahead of yourself, especially in moments with a high degree of personal gain and emotional charge, is very difficult. If anyone "earned the right" to continue with his expedition, it was Shackleton. After all, he had failed twice, been fired, and was now about to put it all on the line after years of planning and preparing. On top of that, he was willing to give it all up to fight for England, a country he was not even from (he was Irish). A great leader is consistently willing and able to put the needs of others ahead of what he wants or needs. A great leader will trust that if he or she does so, *they* will get enough of what they want and need in the long run.

> *One-word telegram to Ernest Shackleton from Winston Churchill: "Proceed."*

And so Shackleton and crew set sail for the Antarctic. After making a stop in Buenos Aires they departed for the island of South Georgia. They stock up on supplies and soon were ready to brave the Southern Ocean, the roughest ocean on the planet. It was reported by local fisherman that the ice in this particular year, 1914, was thicker than average. Several people warned Shackleton about this, expressing their concern for his safety. Despite the warnings and concerns from some, Shackleton decided to push southward.

The plan was to arrive at Vahsel Bay and set up camp before the winter set in. Just 20 miles from their goal, the ship, named Endurance, became stuck in the ice. They were not in danger at this point. In fact, many previous polar expeditions had experienced this. The ships were built to withstand a lot of pressure from the ice. However, the Endurance was stuck, and there was little that they could do. After some time, Shackleton ordered the men to depart the ship.

The crew tried to solve the problem by sawing through the ice. "We're stuck in the ice, so let's cut through it and free the ship." They put forth a Herculean effort. The ice was nearly 20 feet thick. Their goal was on target but the reality of the situation was such that success would be impossible. It's like a guy standing on the roof of his house with a garden hose taking on a raging forest fire. But given the circumstances, what choice did the men have?

Let's transpose this into our world. There are many times when we are moving forward and all of a sudden our ship becomes "stuck in the ice," meaning our progress is suddenly halted. Many circumstances beyond our control can cause our ships to become stuck in the ice. Think about the economy, the competition, and other factors beyond your control. There are too many to list, but you know what they are.

The question for us is the same one faced by the men of the Endurance team. When the ship becomes stuck, what do we do? If we are like Shackleton's men, there is a knee-jerk reaction to remedy the situation immediately, and so we begin "sawing our ship out of the ice" with the hope that it will become free. Sometimes the responses we think will work are spot-on, but sometimes they are way off. In the case of Shackleton's team, they were way off. Although at first glance their efforts appeared to be paying off. However they soon realized that new ice was forming faster than they could cut, poke, slice, and remove it.

After exhausting themselves with saws and poles trying to free the ship, Shackleton ordered the men to stop. After a while he says something like, "Let's stop working, and start playing." The men probably thought that their leader was crazy. Shackleton then tossed a soccer ball out onto the ice.

You're thinking, "What?? Why would Shackleton do this? That won't free the ship! They're stuck in the middle of the Weddell Sea. If they don't get the ship free, they'll never get out of there alive. Playing games won't free the ship. They should try to saw harder and faster! They should go around to the other side! Maybe they can use dynamite and blast their way out!"

It's true that they'd never have gotten out alive without a ship in open waters. No way they could have swum home. Even Michael Phelps couldn't do that! However, the idea to engage the men in a soccer game reflects a flash of brilliance by Shackleton.

Shackleton recognized that they were threatened by the ice, by the cold temperatures, and by the scarcity of food. However, these were not the biggest threats.

Shackleton figured out that the greatest threat his men were facing was not physical, but rather mental. In particular Shackleton's case, he knew that it was critical that his men stay focused, always thinking ahead. Keeping the minds of people continually moving forward in any difficult situation is often the difference between success and failure.

I didn't say that the ice, ship and other factors were not a threat! I said they were not the *biggest* threats. Engaging the men in a soccer game was a remedy to address the mental and emotional threats.

For a leader, one of the most important factors in overcoming difficulties when the "ship becomes stuck in the ice" is to identify the biggest threat, and then to initiate the appropriate action. Here is a key to getting it right: Sometimes the biggest threat is not what is visible or obvious. When facing a serious problem, great leaders don't react too quickly; they take the time to understand the difference between the symptoms and the causes. They realize that people become very disengaged when attacking symptoms, never getting to the causes. If we spend our time, resources, and energy "sawing ships from the ice", facing little chance of success, we risk burn-out for ourselves and our people. We waste time, money and energy—and we risk disengaging our people.

How do you respond when your ship becomes stuck in the ice?

These photos also teach us is the importance of separating what you *can* control from what you *cannot*
control. Look at the goal post in the photo. You see
how it separates the ship from the soccer game? This
is very significant on a metaphorical level. The ship
is an example of something the men have no control
over. As good as they are and as hard as they try, that
ship is *not* going to move. The soccer game represents

something they have full control over. They can decide to play or not to play.

Here's the point for us: Separating what we have full control over (the soccer game) from what we have zero control over (the ship being stuck) is critical for leaders to understand. When people waste time "sawing ships from the ice," they are wasting a lot of time, energy and mental hard-drive space. And, they're wasting mental hard-drive space.

Time, energy and mental capacity are all limited resources, and they are all necessary to the success of your endeavor. Don't waste them on things you can't control! Invest them in things that you *can* control, to make the biggest impact. One of the fastest ways to disengage people from doing quality work is to have them spinning their wheels on matters they have little or no control over, making minimal if any progress.

As I travel and speak to many companies in various industries around the world, I hear horror stories every week related to this matter. When a boss puts a workload on someone that they have little control over, the worker becomes very discouraged and disengaged. When performance reviews and compensation bonuses are tied to factors that workers have little to no control over, they become disengaged, and cynical. The Gallup Group calls this "actively disengaged." These are just a few examples of how costly it is to organizations when people waste time "sawing ships from the ice." Worse yet, their performance is rated on too many issues that they have little or no control over. It's very costly to businesses in many ways when people waste time "sawing ships from the ice."

In order to get the most mileage from this point, here's a suggestion. Find a copy of this photo and blow it up to an 8 x 10 size. (If you'd like a high resolution digital copy of the soccer game photo, please email me.) Print the picture, frame it, and hang it somewhere in your workspace where you'll see it regularly. Tell your people the story and the point of the story. Every time they see this picture they'll be consciously reminded to spend their time and energy wisely on matters that they can control, and let the others go. Helping people spend their time wisely on important matters is a hallmark of a great leader. Shackleton led the way for us in this matter.

> *"Difficulties are just things to overcome."*
>
> — **ERNEST SHACKLETON**

THE IMPORTANCE OF RECOGNITION & REWARD

While there were many factors beyond his control, there were also many that *were* in Shackleton's control. Of those that he could control it was critical that he got those right.

One of the factors that Shackleton had full control over was how to reward and recognize his people. He knew that the morale and spirit of his men was a critical factor in keeping them focused, working together and moving forward, no matter what the Antarctic threw at them. Whether it was on a micro-scale (recognizing the individual) or on a macro-scale (recognizing the group), Shackleton clearly understood the importance of people feeling appreciated, validated and recognized.

Shackleton continually took measures to make sure that his teammates were recognized and rewarded in ways that were meaningful and timely. The journals are full of examples demonstrating this as a pattern.

Here's an example of how Shackleton did this. In the photo below, they were half-way through the four-month period of darkness, so Shackleton decided to celebrate the upcoming return of the sun. This was significant and meaningful to the crew of the

Endurance. And this is just one example of many ways that Shackleton made his people feel recognized and special. If you read through the journals of the crew, you'll hear them tell of many, many times when Shackleton specifically made special efforts for them, both individually and collectively, to really make them feel appreciated.

Great leaders understand the importance of recognizing and rewarding their team members.

It's important to understand this celebration was *not* someone's birthday, Christmas or New Year's Day. This was a holiday that Shackleton created simply to recognize and reward his people in a timely manner. He called it the Mid-Winter's Day celebration. You see, in the Antarctic winter, it's dark for nearly four months at this time of the year due to the curvature and tilt of the earth. The darkness and depression were enemies that Shackleton's crew had to contend with.

Recognizing and rewarding people properly is the key to getting them to *want* to work for you. And the only way to get people to produce superior work is to get them to *want* to do it of their own accord. Nobody can make them. It has to come from within themselves. When people feel appreciated and validated, they are much more likely to reciprocate and want to work hard for you and your company. Shackleton clearly understood this.

People today need to feel appreciated and recognized, too. It keeps them inspired, focused, and on top of their game. The Gallup organization conducted a fascinating study to discover the importance of recognizing and rewarding people, and to assess its correlation to how engaged they were in their jobs. Gallup conducted a 20-year study, from 1980 to 2000, in which they interviewed millions of front-line employees and hundreds of thousands of managers and leaders. The purpose of the study was to better understand what causes people to stay with a company or to leave. In other words, what engaged them and caused them to want to plant their roots.

A major conclusion of the study was that the world's best leaders *all* demonstrated a particular pattern of activities that made them more effective. Gallup discovered 12 attributes that predicted which leaders would be truly effective. When employees gave positive responses to 12 specific yes-or-no questions, it indicated that their managers were superior leaders.

One of those questions was: "In the past seven days, have I been recognized or praised for good work done?" In other words, the need for people to be appreciated and validated regularly is clear.

When you look at how Shackleton led his crew, he regularly made genuine efforts to recognize and reward his people, both individually and collectively, in ways that were both timely and meaningful.

What about you and *your* team? As *you* look at your team members, how can you recognize and reward them (both individually and collectively) in ways that are timely and meaningful? What can you do for people that would really make them feel special? What impact do you think this will have on them? Their co-workers? Your customers? What about your reputation that is generated on-and-offline as a result?

Recognizing and rewarding people in ways that are timely and meaningful is the hallmark of a great leader. Shackleton set us the example in this area. The impact of doing this pay dividends in many ways.

CREATIVE EXAMPLES OF RECOGNITION & REWARDS

The best leaders are very creative when it comes to recognizing and rewarding people. They make sure that they deliver timely and meaningful experiences for their people, individually and collectively. The first example in on a micro-scale, one person to another. The second example is on a macro-scale, one person to an entire company.

The first is a $25 million manufacturing company in Philadelphia. The CEO told me about Bill, a key employee of his whom he considers to be his right-hand man. Bill had been with the company for many years. Recently, however, he had not been very engaged. He worked more like someone who was merely maintaining the business—instead of trying to grow it. The CEO was at his wit's end, and wondered how he could motivate Bill in a way that would work. He had tried raising his salary; offering incentives; increasing his vacation. None of it worked.

I said, "Let's stop for a minute and put ourselves in Bill's shoes. What is the single most important thing in Bill's life—24/7, on or off the job?"

The CEO thought about it for a moment and said, "His 15-year-old teenage daughter!"

"Okay—Let's think about this for a minute," I said. "Who is her favorite musical performer or band?" I figured I had a high probability of getting a specific answer, as what 15-year-old kid—especially a gal—isn't head-over-heels for some rock star?

"Taylor Swift," he smiled. I could see that he was starting to "get it."

I continued, "What if we set a performance goal for Bill. Let's call it X." I drew a horizontal line across the whiteboard and labeled it "X." "We'll figure out exactly what X is later. If Bill clears this bar, guess where he and his 15-year-old teenage daughter will go next time Taylor is in Philly?"

Startled, he said, "Wow, that's a great idea!"

"Hold on—it gets better," I said. Then his eyes got really big! I drew another horizontal line above the line I had labeled X and put on it's axis "X + Y." "What if Bill clears that bar, "X +Y"?

He paused for a few seconds and said, "Front row seats?"

"Bingo."

Think about what was happening here. The issue was *not* money. Bill is a key employee and makes a good living. If he really wanted to take his daughter to see

Taylor Swift and sit in the front row, he could buy the tickets. However, think about what we really did for Bill in this case. What Bill's boss did for him was make him a *hero* in the eyes his daughter. Yes, made Bill a HERO! How much is *that* worth to Bill? What impact do you think this will have on him? How will it manifest itself in the company? How will other co-workers be impacted? Customers? The company's reputation? You get the idea.

Making someone a hero in the eyes of the most important person or people in their lives will move the employee engagement needle like few things will. Stop for a minute and think about the experiences you've had as an employee. When was the last time that your boss or manager made you feel like a true hero? How many times has this happened to you in your career? Most people I meet tell me that it happens rarely, if ever.

Think about your team members—every single one of them. What would it take to make each of them a hero? What would it take to make them feel so special that they would want to go above and beyond for you and your company? What would be the impact if just one person at your company felt this way? What if two people felt this way? An entire department?

My challenge to you is to pick just one person this week. Think of someone specifically that you can make a hero. Who is that person? What will you do in order to really make them feel like a hero? What do you have to know about them in order to make this happen? Who do you need to speak with in order to find out what will really inspire them in a way they have never been inspired before? As you think about this, remember, it's rarely about money!

Here's an example from my own life when I was made a hero...and it had nothing to do with money.

Back in 2002, I was working as the director of recruiting and training for a SCI, a large publically-traded firm in the cemetery and funeral industry. My job was to help our managers and VP's across America to be more effective in their efforts to recruit and retain sales people. Part of how I accomplished this was by teaching a leadership course called "Managing For Excellence."

This was also about the time that I had recently discovered the story of Shackleton's Endurance expedition. My boss, George Hubbard, knew that I was obsessed with Shackleton. I had just developed a segment of the Managing For Excellence program by using photos to tell Shackleton's story to illustrate the same points. People loved it, as it was my start on a new journey that has led me to writing this book.

Back to my boss George. One day I received a card from him in the mail. By the way, things that actually show up at people's houses in something called mailboxes, have *huge* value. In a world of e-this and instant that, there is something very special and meaningful about sending someone a card or gift that literally shows up at their front door, if only because it's so rare in this day and age.

Just getting a handwritten card from George seemed special, but that was nothing. That was nothing compared to what the note said. I tore open the envelope with great anticipation. I began reading and was stunned. The note said, "Mike, I want to thank you for being my right hand person in our efforts. Just like Shackleton could depend on his right hand guy, Frank Wild, you are very dependable. Mike, you are my Frank Wild."

Just telling this story almost makes me get teary. That was 13 years ago, and the impact is just significant today as it was back then. That card from George is the most special card I've ever gotten from anyone in my life, *ever*. I felt like a true hero thanks to George. He took the time to know what was meaningful to me—and he took action.

George took the time to thank me in a way that was timely and meaningful to me. How much did it cost George? A dollar for the card and stamp, plus a few minutes of his time and thoughts, is not much. However, it meant the world to me. During my time working for George at SCI, I showed up early, stayed late, and went way above and beyond the job description on countless occasions. I wanted to do a great job. How George recognized and rewarded me inspired me to want to do my best, and then some.

> *"Superhuman effort isn't worth a
> damn unless it achieves results."*
>
> — Ernest Shackleton

Here's another example, this one from a speaking engagement I did for a group of CEO's in Los Angeles. We were discussing this same point on recognizing and rewarding people, and I asked for examples from the audience. One of the CEO's stood up and told us a compelling story of how he recognized and rewarded his entire company. As 2011 was coming to a close, and the planning for 2012 was in full gear, he gathered all the employees for a company-wide meeting. This was a fairly small company, with revenue of $5 million. They were an IT company serving large organizations.

Now the backdrop to the story is that the CEO knew that what inspired a large segment of his workforce were three charities that were near and dear to them. How did he know this? He *asked*. It's amazing what you discover about people when you stop, ask really good questions, and listen carefully to what they say. He developed a plan to financially support their charities, and he tied it to performance measures.

So he drew four horizontal lines on a flip chart and labeled them 1%, 2%, 3% and 4% respectively, from the bottom up. He explained, "If we get to this line of revenue for 2012, I'll contribute 1% of every dollar we generate to the three charities, in all of your names. If we get to this line, I'll contribute 2%, and so on—up to the maximum at the top line of 4%."

Where do you think they finished up the year 2012? It was a record breaking year measured by revenue. They cleared the top line, and the CEO wrote a check at the end of that year for $40,000 to the three charities, in the names of all his employees. The CEO went on to explain that every metric in the firm improved.

Tying people's performance to rewards that mean something to them is a highly effective way to get them to perform better. On top of that, it transformed the culture into one where people *wanted* to push themselves and excel. Keep in mind that none of his employees received a dime. It was all about the charities that were important to them.

One thing this example shows us is that rewards that are important to people are not always measured in ways that come back directly to themselves—those rewards sometimes go to *others*. The rewards that are important to people may not be what you assume they are. This is why asking and listening to what matters to people is so important. Great leaders do this consistently.

Recognizing and rewarding people, both individually and collectively, is a very powerful and effective way to engage people. It impacts every aspect of the quality of your people, from finding them to keeping them. It impacts the relationships you build with customers, vendors and partners. In addition, your future pool of employees, customers, and others will also be affected.

> *"He [Shackleton] led mentally and physically and gave a sense to the individual that he, the individual, was a most important part of the whole show."*
>
> — GIBERT DOUGLAS,
> ANTARCTIC GEOLOGIST

As you think about your team and how engaged they are, or are not, remember this: You can't *make* people do anything, yet alone things that are really difficult. People have to want to do this of their own accord.

Paying people, pleading with them, and threatening them only go so far. To go further, they have to *want* to do this. Great leaders get people to *want* to go that extra mile. Recognizing and rewarding them in ways that are timely and meaningful is a great way to accomplish this.

One of the most effective ways to get people to go above-and-beyond—to give 110%—is to recognize and reward them in ways that are both timely and meaningful to them.

LEADING BY EXAMPLE

Okay, the men of the Endurance expedition are stuck in the ice-pack and drifting aimlessly in the Weddell Sea. There is nothing they can do except wait it out and hope for a break in the ice. Despite the fact that there was little within their control, Shackleton still found opportunities to lead his men effectively. Here's an example from this picture.

Shackleton never expected his men to do anything he wasn't willing and able to do first

While it appears that it's just a man peering through a telescope at night during a very cold winter night, it's much more than that. That man is Ernest Shackleton. What he is doing is keeping an eye on the ice. They called this the "all-night watch." During the long polar nights, every night, someone had to stay up and

keep watch. You may ask, "Why? Watch for what?" For the killer penguins, of course! Seriously though, the men had to watch for any movement in the ice.

Imagine their situation: These guys were not on solid ground. There were on giant ice floes that were floating in the middle of the ocean. This was a very dangerous and dynamic environment. The ice shits, moves, cracks, and gives way; and, it's completely unpredictable. It is acted-upon by the powerful-yet-invisible forces of the ocean beneath.

For the Endurance crew, this meant that at any time, gaping holes in the ice could appear right beneath them! Someone had to watch for movement or any other threats to the men, like attacks from leopard seals.

This illustrates another hallmark of Ernest Shackleton as a leader. He was always willing to volunteer for the difficult jobs.Most people would not expect that a task like this would be carried out by the expedition leader! No, this would be a job done by a less-experienced or a lower-level crew person, not Shackleton. Unfortunately, this is too often the case in many organizations. It is rare to see the senior staff in too many organizations doing the dirty grunt work. Shackleton never asked or expected his crew members to do anything that he himself was not willing and able to do first. He knew that his *actions* spoke louder and carried much more weight than his *words*.

In fact, this inspired the men as much as almost anything else that Shackleton did. If you read through the 27 crewmen's journals, you'll see that many of them wrote about Shackleton being first to volunteer for the all-night watch. This says a lot!

What about your leadership? What can you do on the job that will set an example for your people? Ask yourself what Shackleton might do in your position. What parts of the job could you be doing personally that would inspire your people?

You may have heard the expression, "Where the leaders lead, the people follow." This is as true today as it was in Antarctica 100 years ago. Leaders who personally do the things at work that are not glamorous, fun, or get easily noticed are often the most important. Your example speaks louder than your words. People will be willing to go as far as the leaders. If you want people to push farther, then go farther *yourself.* Ask yourself, "What can I do that will set a more powerful example for others around me?" Write it down and make a specific commitment to doing it *today.*

"He did not care if he went without a shirt on his own back, so long as the men he was leading had sufficient clothing. He was a wonderful man in that way; the men in the party mattered more than anything else."

— LIONEL GREENSTREET, FIRST OFFICER, ENDURANCE

FROM INCONVENIENCE TO SACRIFICE

It is now the autumn of 1915. The Endurance crew is not in imminent danger; rather, they are inconvenienced. They are simply waiting for the ice to melt and loosen its grip on the ship, so they can resume their voyage. The Good News is that the ice starts to melt. The Bad News is that the weight of the ice causes the ship to list.

"What the ice gets, the ice keeps."

Soon thereafter the ship to gave way to the pressure and was crushed like a toy truck under an elephant's foot.

As Shackleton said, "What the ice gets, the ice keeps."

Now the crew of the Endurance is in trouble. They're stranded on an ice floe in the middle of the Weddell Sea, drifting away from land. Before the Endurance sank, the men managed to pull off some supplies and three life rafts. At this point Shackleton set up camp on the ice, and appropriately named it "Camp Patience." Not much else they could do at this point but wait for a break in the ice, which would allow them to launch the life rafts.

Shackleton then gathered his men together in a semi-circle to address them. He stared intensely into their eyes. His exact words were not recorded—apparently their iPhones stopped functioning at 30 degrees below zero—but in essence he said, "Okay guys, now the game has changed. Our goal is no longer to trek across Antarctica. The new goal is for us to get home alive!"

"In order to increase our chances of survival, I'm limiting each man to carrying only two pounds of personal possessions. Period." This was much harder for the men than it may seem. Consider that they had photographs, musical instruments, books, costumes, personal mementos, memorable gifts, and other creature comforts.

As was his custom, Shackleton went first in discarding his personal items, setting the example for his men. He never expected them to do anything that he himself was not willing to do first. In front of his men, he threw out onto the ice gold coins and a fine pocket watch that someone had given him as a gift. Then, he tossed a Bible onto the ice, a Bible that the Queen of England had signed to the men of the Endurance! This was very difficult for Shackleton, and something that had a powerful impact on his men.

After the entire crew made many difficult decisions, and had tossed many personal and meaningful items out onto the ice, Shackleton looked at his men and said words to this effect: "If you think *that* was difficult you haven't seen *anything* yet. Discarding our personal possessions is hard—it's called inconvenience. However, if we're going to make it out alive, we're going to have to go to the next level—it's called *sacrifice*." Great leaders understant that there's a big difference between inconvenience and sacrifice.

With a sad, drawn face he silently turned his head to the left...and stared at the dogs.

After a pause that must have seemed like hours to his men, Shackleton said, "Yes, they're next."

And this is where inconvenience turns into sacrifice.

Shackleton called for true sacrifice by ordering all dogs be put down

The men of the Endurance were going to have to put down all the dogs that had been their beloved companions for months, including four puppies that were born on the trip. Shackleton insisted that each man put down his own dogs. As a leader, he knew that he had to get his men personally involved in anything pertaining to their survival their very survival. Shackleton knew that his entire crew had to *participate* in this heart-wrenching activity.

Personally speaking, this is a very difficult story for me to tell. I'm an animal lover. On May 23, 2011, my wife Angela and I had to put our cat, Sebastian, down. He had been with us for 18 years. I bet I cried for a month. As hard as this story of sacrifice is to tell and hear, think about how difficult it was for

Shackleton and his men. If you're like most people, you're asking WHY did Shackleton have to do this? One simple reason: food. The amount of food that it took to feed both the men *and* the dogs for one *day*, would feed the men alone for one *week*.

This is yet another example of how Shackleton demonstrated his leadership qualities. He remained objective in a circumstance that had a high degree of emotional charge. He made a sound decision that was in the best interest of the team, regardless of how they felt or what the outcome of a popular vote would have been.

Making difficult decisions that are critical to the team when you're in a situation with a high degree of risk and emotional charge is very hard for the vast majority of leaders. Let's face it: Anyone can make an important decision when there is not much on the line and the level of emotional charge is low. However, when there is a lot on the line and the level of emotional charge is high, it's very difficult to stay objective and make the right decision. It separates those who merely *look* like leaders from those who truly *are* leaders.

The dogs were important to the men for many reasons, including companionship, transport help and possibly a food source. In this case, as well as in the world of business, we know that every asset comes at a price. For Shackleton and his men, the cost of feeding the dogs was not worth risking the well-being of the crew. For us, we have to think long and hard about every asset we have at our disposal to do the best work possible.

> *"Great leaders understand the difference between inconvenience and sacrifice."*
>
> — ANTARCTIC MIKE

Just like Shackleton, leaders today have many assets at their disposal to grow their businesses. We have employees, materials, machines, time, ideas, intellectual property and capital to move our companies forward. An important question that we need to ask ourselves is this: Are we making sound and objective decisions about how to use those assets most effectively? As leaders, we sometimes have to make very difficult decisions to sacrifice things that are near and dear to our hearts. We must do this in order to move our businesses forward and do the right thing for the good of the group—whether that's your employees, customers or any other group your business is associated with.

Most CEO's I speak to see "shooting the dogs" as analogous to having to let people go. Most leaders who have had to fire people will tell you this is never easy. This is even harder when you have to let go of someone you like and respect. Since the economic crash of 2008, I've met business owners and executives every week who tell me that the economy is like a game of Musical Chairs in which they simply have to let someone go. When that person or group of people are being let go for reasons other than discipline or poor performance, it's really difficult. However, as a leader you are responsible for making the best decisions for the team, not just for any one person.

CEO's tell me that one of the very hardest "dogs to put down" is what I call the "legacy employee." This is the person who's been with you for a very long time; you like them—a lot! However, after a certain period of time, you notice that he or she is not as engaged as they used to be. For one reason or another, either the job has changed, the person has changed, or circumstances have changed, and he or she is no longer fully engaged. You have a right shoe on a left foot. It's just not a good fit.

Think about this: If you switched your shoes, putting the right shoe on your left foot and vice versa, and you started walking down the street, how long would it take until it was obvious to you that something simply was not right? Not long I'll bet. Not only would *you* know it, but everyone *around* you would clearly see that something was wrong. In the business world many things that are "simply not right" are perfectly obvious to other employees, vendors, and even customers.

Let me give you an example of how *not* removing the wrong person can have serious consequences. About six months ago I received a call from one of my customers. I had placed "Sally" in a small Texas company a few years ago. She was a top performing salesperson.

"Mike, I need some advice!" She sounded frantic. "My team and I just got out of a major presentation to our biggest client. After the meeting the firm's CEO took me aside and said, 'I'm going to be blunt here. We love your firm and your products. But if you don't remove *Joe* from this equation entirely, we're going to write a check to another company. Have I made myself perfectly clear? Mike...Joe is our VP of Sales!"

Can you imagine having that conversation?? How would *you* react if your biggest client said this about your firm and one of your colleagues?

Sally gave me further background on the hapless VP: He'd been a sales guy for nearly 20 years. However, Joe was *not* a leader. He was a great individual contributor, but he was *not* a *leader*. His promotion was based on a variety of factors—none of which had anything to do with his leadership abilities.

Unfortunately, this happens all the time in the business world.

The more I meet with companies and hear stories, the more convinced I am that way too many leaders and managers got their positions like many people became parents. They woke up one day and there was a status change. Someone put a hat on them that said LEADER, and dumped a load on them called leadership...with no instructions on how to carry that load. Many of these leaders know that something is wrong, but they don't say anything because they don't want to upset their boss, or lose their job.

Way too many people become leaders because they are great individual contributors, they have long tenure, are well liked, they look good, smell good and are in the right place at the right time. None of these things have any correlation to actually doing the job of leading other people.

Oh, and here's how Sally's story played out. For several months she and her team shielded the customer from Joe. Finally Joe was let go. *And*...three weeks later Joe's boss, the CEO, resigned.

Making hard decisions to "shoot the dogs" is never easy for anyone. This is what separates those who *look* like a leader from those who really *are* a leader.

Great leaders never let the diffiulty or emotions of a situation stop them from making the right decisions. Ernest Shackleton was this leader.

> *"I know for a fact that he did not once lie down for three days and I don't think he has undressed for ten days. He seems always on the alert, especially at night, having certainly been up every night for the last three weeks."*
>
> — Thomas Orde-Lees, Endurance Crew Member

REDEFINING "PERSISTENT"

At this point Shackleton realized that the men had to get out of there before winter came. If they did not get to solid land, there would be no chance of survival. What they needed was a break in the ice in order to launch the lifeboats. They had pulled three of them off the Endurance before she had been crushed and sunk. In April, 1916, they got the break they needed, as there was (literally) a break in the ice that allowed them to launch the life boats.

For seven seemingly endless days and nights all 28 men fought for their lives aboard the three small boats. They finally ended up on remote Elephant Island—a small, uninhabited island among the chain of islands arcing up toward the tip of South America from Antarctica.

For the first time in 497 days the men were finally on *land*. That's the Good News. The Bad News: No one in the outside world knew where they were. They weren't in a shipping lane, and Elephant Island didn't have wi-fi. There wouldn't be a drive-by or fly over!

It's now late March of 1916. Winter is on its way. Shackleton knew that they couldn't survive on Elephant Island for long. So he made another difficult decision. Being the courageous leader he was, he and five men left Elephant Island to get help. One of the five guys he chose was Timothy McNeish, their carpenter. Timothy was the most difficult and hard-headed person on the crew of 27. Why did Shackleton choose McNeish? Yes, he needed him in the lifeboat for his carpentry skills, but he also didn't want to "pawn off his difficult employee onto his manager," Frank Wild. One of the consistent aspects of Shackleton's story is how he continually took personal responsibility for the difficult jobs as well as the difficult people—and also for the unexpected situations that would regularly crop up. Shackleton and the others left the remaining 22 men behind on Elephant Island under the command of Frank Wild, Shackleton's right-hand man.

17 days and nights crossing the Southern Ocean

Shackleton and his team of five set sail in the *James Caird*, a 23-foot dinghy. Their goal was to sail to the island of South Georgia, some 800 miles away. This was the only reasonable destination due to the high winds and the strong currents of the Southern Ocean, the roughest sea on the planet. For 17 days and nights, they fought and struggled for their lives. The non-stop battle against 60-foot waves is an amazing story within the larger story. Due to bad weather, they couldn't even get a navigational reading on their location for days.

Long story short . . . miraculously . . . Shackleton and his men reached South Georgia 17 days later. That was the good news. The bad news was that they had beached on the wrong—uninhabited—side of the island. The Worse News was that because the near-hurricane conditions had broken the mast off their boat, they could not sail around to the other side.

Again, leading by example, Shackleton and two others went for help. They hiked almost 30 miles in 36 non-stop hours, crossing the 5,000-foot mountain peaks. Nobody had ever ventured more than one mile into the interior of South Georgia. And, of course, they did not have a map, GPS, a planned route to follow.

That, in-and-of itself, would be a daunting task for anyone. But don't forget, this was after spending 17 days and nights in a 23-foot dinghy sailing the world's roughest ocean; and that's after being stranded at sea for 497 days; and *that* followed sailing 12,000 miles from England on the dawn of World War I! Under such conditions of duress, it's amazing that Shackleton could continue moving forward; mentally, emotionally, and physically.

> *"Even when you fall on your face,*
> *you're moving forward."*
>
> —Victor Kiam

Shackleton and his two comrades successfully traversed South Georgia Island. They found the small whaling station and sent a rescue crew back to save the others who had been left behind on South Georgia Island. Remember, Shackleton had left 22 men behind under the command of Frank Wild. Because it was winter (April 1916), it took four attempts—four!—to rescue to the men back on South Georgia due to impassable ice. In August, 1916, they finally made it back to Elephant Island, where all 22 men were still alive!

It's amazing that all of Shackleton's men survived for nearly two years in the harshest environment on earth. Certainly the team had a few lucky breaks that were beyond their control, and that contributed to their survival. However, there were also plenty of factors within their control that required great decision making and strong leadership thinking. Shackleton demonstrated time and time again that he was a great leader.

From the start, Shackleton had the vision to do what nobody else had ever thought of or tried. He picked the right men for the job and clearly defined their roles in a way that they understood.He listened to his men intently. He knew what drove them, individually and collectively. He recognized and rewarded them in ways that were timely and meaningful. He inspired his men to want to continue to push non-stop, and he got the best from every one of them. In just about every way, Shackleton was the poster child of a great leader.

What about you? What decisions will you make that will inspire your people to want to be better, be more focused and get better results? What characteristics in Shackleton's life do you want to emulate? How will this make a difference in the performance of your team? Why will it matter?

THE POWER OF PASSION

Just a few short years after this, in 1920, Shackleton was not finished as an explorer. He organized a *fourth* journey to the Antarctic—the Quest Expedition. What this says about Shackleton is that being an explorer is not *what he did*, but rather *who he was*. Exploring was not his *job*; it was his *passion*.

Speaking of passion...Harvard University conducted a survey in 1960. Fifteen-hundred MBA graduates were asked:

As you build your lives and careers, which of these two roads would you choose to follow?

1. Road #1 Get your financial house in order first, then pursue what you love to do.

2. Road #2 Pursue what you love to do and trust that all your needs will come as a result of doing what you love.

Ninety-two percent of them (1,280) chose Road #1—getting their house in order first. Only eight percent (120) of them chose Road #2—pursuing what they loved first.

Twenty years later in 1980, there was a class reunion for the 1,500 graduates. In this group, there were 101 millionaires.

Here's the question: How many millionaires chose Road #1, and how many chose Road #2? [Pause here for reflection.] Only one of the 101 millionaires had followed Road #1—to get their house in order first. A hundred of them had followed Road #2—to pursue what they loved first. These people followed their passion and trusted that everything they needed would come as a result.

The moral of the story is obvious: The power of passion and doing what you love to do should never be underestimated. Shackleton wasn't a Harvard MBA, but he was a man who was driven by passion and purpose. This is a big reason why he was successful and considered by many to be one of the greatest leaders to have ever lived.

Bringing this into today's world, think of the late Steve Jobs from Apple. Developing iPads, iTunes, iPhones and i-everything-else was not merely what he did. It was who he was. He couldn't *not* do it. Leaders today have a responsibility to help their people understand who they really are before they put them in a particular seat on the bus. Aligning people's talents and true motivations with the deliverables and expectations of the job is one of the most important tasks that great leaders get right.

SHACKLETON PLANS HIS FOURTH EXPEDITION

Back to Shackleton; once again he began assembling a new crew for the Quest Expedition, his fourth trip to the Antarctic.

Quick question: Wouldn't you think that the men of the Endurance Expedition, having failed in their initial mission, and having to fight for their lives for two years, would never, *ever* want to venture anywhere near Antarctica?! Amazingly, 7 of the 27 men who struggled with Shackleton signed up voluntarily and enthusiastically to be members of his new expedition. This really sheds light on the superior type of leader that Shackleton was, and on the impact he had on his men.

During the planning of the Quest Expedition one of Shackleton's old friends and crewmates—and a doctor aboard the *Endurance*—Alexander Macklin, pulled Shackleton aside one day. He said, "Listen, Ernest, you're now 47 years old. You've had a heart attack, and you have a wife and kids at home who need you. You *have* to give this up!"

Shackleton looked calmly at him and slowly shook his head. Being an explorer was not *what he did*—it was *who he was.* He simply didn't know any other way.

That conversation with Macklin was one of the last he ever had with anyone. The next day, at 2:30am on January 5, 1922, Ernest Shackleton suffered a massive heart attack and died. It was a sudden and sad ending to the life of one of the greatest leaders the world has ever known.

The last surviving member of the Endurance crew was Lionel Greenstreet, who lived until 1979. He lived an amazingly long life. Just before he died, he was interviewed and asked about the Endurance Expedition. A reporter asked him, "Lionel, many of these polar expeditions failed, and many people lost their lives. Yours, however, was successful. What made the difference?"

Lionel looked at him, and after a long pause he said one word: "Shackleton."

Think about this for a minute. This interview was conducted many decades after the *Endurance* expedition, many years after Shackleton died. I believe if Lionel had lived to be 500 years old he would have answered the question in the exact same way, and in the same tone of voice.

The impact Shackleton left on his men was permanent. *When leaders lead properly, the mark they leave on people is indelible.* It does not have an expiration date or a shelf life. The message they write on the minds and hearts of people is permanent. Ernest Shackleton and the men of the Endurance changed the course of history and the lives of many people forever.

No, you weren't alive in 1914, and your business does not involve going to Antarctica to cross the continent. However, why should we think for one minute that we don't have the same opportunity—and responsibility—to help our people change the course of history and their lives forever, through what they do for a living.

> *"When leaders lead people properly, the mark they leave on people is indelible."*
> — ANTARCTIC MIKE

Think about this for a minute. Every single one of your employees is giving you the very best hours of their lives. They rise at five or six in the morning, in the dark; they fight traffic and show up first thing. They spend all day until five or six or later; they leave in the dark and fight traffic again; they return home home beat up. They do this for you day in and day out. We owe it to them to help them be better people, not just better employees. That's what great leaders do. That's what Shackleton did. What will *you* do?

Lionel Greenstreet, the last surviving member of the Endurance crew

"No words can do justice to their courage and their cheerfulness. To be brave cheerily, to be patient with a glad heart, to stand the agonies of thirst with laughter and song, to walk beside death for months and never be sad; that's the spirit that makes courage worth having. I loved my men."

— ERNEST SHACKLETON

FOLLOWING IN SHACKLETON'S FOOTSTEPS

Now that I've taken you through Shackleton's story, and you've seen what a great leader he was, I'm confident you can see why I was drawn to this story.

Let's go back to 2003. Thanks to "downsizing," I lost my job with SCI. While most people thought this was really Bad News, it was actually Good News in disguise. For the next few years I gained a broader range of business experience through a variety of sales jobs—while laying the groundwork for my speaking business.

I never lost sight of my goal to become a full-time professional speaker and share the Shackleton story with many companies. But I didn't have a clue about how to go about this. Well, as I relatd earlier, I discovered the National Speakers Association, which led to meeting that Godek character who convinced me that I had to actually *go* to Antarctica. So I signed up. I was now committed.

Now what??

Sports-talk radio hosts Scott and BR, of the Mighty 1090 in San Diego

ON THE AIR—WITH "ANTARCTIC MIKE"!

A few weeks after signing-up, in March 2005, Angela and I decided to celebrate my 40th birthday at the Sandbar, a favorite sports bar in Pacific Beach, California. Influencing our decision was a $40 gift certificate that I'd recently won from The Mighty 1090, my favorite local sports-talk radio station. Since I had just spent a ton of money signing up for the Antarctic Marathon, $40 was now a big deal.

At the Sandbar, I met Billy Ray Smith (aka BR) from the "Scott and BR Show," the most popular AM morning sports-talk radio show on the Mighty 1090. I told him my story about heading to Antarctica, and—no pun intended—he said, "Wow that's cool!" He handed me his business card and said, "Hey, give me a call on Monday—I'd love to hear more about this and talk with you about it!"

On Monday I waited—impatiently, I'll admit—two full hours before I called. I was up early that morning and called the station just after 7:00am. When the gal answered the phone, I realized that the number on BR's business card was the on-air number, not an office number. I thought I was calling just to talk with BR, not go live on a radio show. I had never called a radio station before or been on the air.

"I'm sorry, sir, but the guys aren't taking call-ins today," said the firm-but-professional gal who answered the phone. I then realized that the phone number I'd called on BR's business card was the *on-air* number.

"But BR is expecting my call!" I could hear the receptionist's eyes rolling heavenward. *"It's just another rabid fan calling, trying to wheedle his way into his 15-minutes of fame."*

I could feel this opportunity slipping between my fingers. I considered telling her the whole story of my chat with BR, and about Antarctica, and about Shackleton, and about the upcoming marathon. But my smarter self stopped me. I was panicking. How could I say something intriguing-yet-short, something that would grab both her attention and BR's?!

Somehow these words came out of my mouth: "Please, just put the word 'Antarctic' in front of my name Mike. Please tell him that 'Antarctic Mike' is on the line. He'll remember me and might take my call."

I held my breath.

The receptionist sighed, then said, "Okay *Antarctic Mike*. Please hold."

So I waited. And waited. And waited. The line never went dead, so I kept on holding. For 10 minutes. Twenty minutes. Thirty minutes. Instead of Muzak in the background, they played whatever show the radio station was currently broadcasting. I could hear my favorite radio hosts bantering as usual. Suddenly I heard BR's partner Scott Kaplan say, "Hey, BR! We got some guy on hold who calls himself *Antarctic Mike*. What do you think—"

BR broke in, "Put him on! I met him last Saturday. You're not gonna believe what this guy—" and then there was a loud click on the phone line, and I was live on-air, on my favorite radio show, with my favorite DJs. I somehow condensed my story into five minutes, and somehow I was coherent. I certainly was enthusiastic…and apparently entertaining. I guess I did okay, because "Scott & BR" had me back on the air several times in the next few months!

I had just told my story—my dream—to hundreds of thousands of people. The station—with its 50,000-watt blowtorch of a signal—reaches all of Southern California. Plus, Scott & BR had one of the biggest morning audiences of any sports talk radio station in America.

Was I nervous? Hell no!! I love talking to people—this was just a slightly bigger audience than I usually addressed!

When I hung-up the phone I was kind of stunned. I looked over to see Angela smiling at me. "Well... *Antarctic Mike*...You can't back-out now, because a gazillion people just heard you say you're gonna run a marathon in Antarctica." She gave me a hug. Then she walked away, smiling and shaking her head slowly, and repeating, "Antarctic Mike...Antarctic Mike...Hello, I'd like to introduce you to my husband—Antarctic Mike!"

She was right! I realized that I was now accountable to many thousands of people. This was a great lesson in accountability for me. So here's an idea for you if you ever want to take accountability to a whole new level: Choose a difficult goal—one that will not only stretch you, but scare you. Then get on the radio, or make a speech to your entire company, or shout it from the rooftops! You'll now have lots of people who will keep you accountable!

THE FREEZER

After I had wired my $20,000 entry fee to the marathon organizer in Ireland, and officially committed myself to running in the first-ever Antarctic Ice Marathon, it hit me. "I really *am* going to Antarctica!" There was no turning back now. I was excited, nervous—and, to tell the truth, a little fearful—all at the same time. This was early March of 2005. The Marathon would take place in early January of 2006, so I had nine months to prepare. There was plenty of time, but what should I do first?

I pondered this for a while, and then I got smart and asked myself, "What would Shackleton do?" The answer came instantly: *Prepare!*

In order to prepare for the marathon in Antarctica, I spent nearly a year training inside a commercial freezer in San Diego. You would think, as I did, that the value of the freezer was to acclimate to the cold temperatures. While this is true, the real value of the freezer had little to do with cold temperatures and conditioning the body physically. Rather, it had to do with conditioning the mental muscles. And it turns out that the application to the business world was far more valuable than I had ever expected. Here's the story.

After I hung-up with Scott and BR I thought to myself, "Now what??"

"How do I train for this? What do I eat? What do I wear? How do I acclimate to the sub-zero temperatures awaiting me in Antarctica?"

I thought to myself, "I've got to find a freezer! But where?" So I decided to do what any logical person in San Diego who's going to Antarctica would do. He'd start making calls. So I got out the Yellow Pages and started calling every number listed under the word "freezer."

I received only a few return calls from my efforts. They were mostly dead-ends.

"We only make ice."

"We sell refrigeration equipment."

"Are you crazy?"

And finally, "I can't help you, but I know who can." Hallelujah!

John managed a local ice company, so he knew the biz and he knew the players. "We often use Miramar Cold Storage; they have the biggest freezer in San Diego. Call Tibor, the owner. Tell him I referred you."

Great! A major step in the right direction.

Enthusiastically I called Tibor's office. Jennifer fielded my call, but she was friendly—and after I explained my upcoming adventure and my need for a track-sized freezer, she was fired-up. "If it were up to me, I'd hand you a key, Antarctic Mike! But I don't have authority to do that. You need to call Josh. He's the VP."

I left several messages for Josh over the next few days. He didn't return any of my calls. I was a bit disheartened. Then I thought, "What would Shackleton do?" And while I don't know for sure if Shackleton would have come up with the same plan, I'm pretty darn sure that he would have approved.

I decided to just show-up at Josh's front door. It was early April, 2005. It was a hot, 80-degree day. I dressed in my Antarctic gear— red parka with Eskimo-like hood; thermal pants; heavy hiking boots; and goggles—and I appeared at his office. "Josh, it's Antarctic Mike. I just want you to know that I'm serious about wanting to train in your freezer."

As a salesperson you always have to show-up. But sometimes you have to show-up in an outrageous way in order to make an impact.

Josh was bemused but intrigued. He gave me a tour of the facility. It was not glamorous. The building was a series of vault-like freezers, each set to a different temperature, depending on what was stored in each one. I was eager to see "Box #9," as this was the coldest (minus 15 to minus 20 degrees).

Josh had never seen anyone get excited about a freezer, much less ask to run in one! "I'm not the final say, but I'll tell Tibor, the owner, that you're for real, and not crazy!" I was ready to charge into Tibor's office, but Tibor's office was in Pasadena, three hours from San Diego, and he rarely visited his office anymore. Oh, and Tibor was an 80-year-old Hungarian who spoke broken English.

I called. I left messages. I emailed. I tried sending smoke signals. Finally he called me back. It took us a while to bridge the language barrier, but we finally did. I was stunned when he said, "I used to run a business in Antarctica."

What??!!

He explained that he had once owned an engineering firm that built a closed-loop system (don't ask!) that handled all the water and diesel fuel at McMurdo, the largest research facility on the continent. I didn't understand a lot of Tibor's words, but I could definitely feel the excitement in his voice when he talked about Antarctica.

Finally I said, "Tibor, I can tell that were were destined to meet!" He agreed.

...And that's how I found my frozen training center.

This whole experience taught me a valuable business lesson. In order to make things happen, you not only have to be persistent, but you also have to be smart and creative about it. How many sales people leave a commonplace voicemail, and follow-up with a few more, only to get nowhere? The potential client has probably received 200 similarly commonplace and boring calls in the last week alone! Some sales people mail out brochures and other garbage that is predictable and of little or no interest to the recipient.

When I showed-up at Josh's office in full Antarctic gear I didn't simply ask for what I wanted, I showed up with something for him. I explained that in addition to running in his freezer, I wanted to create a charitable event to raise money for a local non-profit organization. The benefit to Miramar Cold Storage would be that the publicity I would generate by running in their freezer would also put Miramar in the spotlight. Josh loved the idea, and that's what convinced him to put me it touch with Tibor.

Here's the takeaway: To be effective in making things happen, don't do what is predictable and boring. Be creative, show up—and when you do so—bring value to the recipient. Don't just pitch what you want. Demonstrate that what you're bringing is of great value to them first! You'll get enough of what you want.

The freezer was a dim, dingy, and cold place. It wasn't like your friendly neighborhood health club! As you can imagine, no crowds here. My private facility was a concrete block rectangle that was 59-feet long. This is the same distance running the football from the 20-yard line into the endzone.

This was my world; every other day for 10 months. I ran hundreds of hours and hundreds of miles in that little 59-foot frozen concrete box...and I LOVED IT!

Was it cold?? Well, yes and no. *Yes*, because temperatures ranging from 10 degrees below zero to 22 degrees below *are* a bit chilly. *No*, because temperatures for our Antarctic marathon would be that cold or colder. Even though it gets down to 90 below zero at the South Pole in the winter, I went in *summer*, so I knew it wouldn't get *that* cold! But one never knows!

Unlike your friendly neighborhood health club, my Miramar Cold Storage facility didn't have flat-screen TVs to keep one distracted. Nor did it have windows or other people to distract me. This was a good thing, because I needed to concentrate.

So I ran back-and-forth, back-and-forth, pounding on the hard concrete floor—for hours. There was no music, no fanfare, no windows to the outside world. Just four cement walls, a hard cement floor, and pallets full of frozen chickens, pizzas, and French fries, stacked to the ceiling. Of course there was the constant roaring of the fans blowing in the minus-20 degree air.

Lots of people tell me that they would have been be bored to death. But I *loved* this place. Really! It was a sanctuary for me. Mostly I ran, but sometimes I sat and rested…and I daydreamed about Antarctica. I would let my mind wander. I thought back 100-years ago and wondered what Shackleton and others felt like being this cold in the middle of nowhere. What was it like to be in a place that was frozen, silent, and more lonely than most people in the world would ever know or experience. The freezer was my opportunity to acclimate to the extreme conditions, and to experience it as closely as possible. So in a way, it was like being in an ice-cold time machine.

Back to my training. Truly, you don't need to be a superhero to do this; most people could acclimate to the cold. If you wear the right gear and keep moving, you can survive. But you have to be focused and driven to keep doing it day after day.

Conditioning the physical and mental muscles in the freezer

But when it's 22 degrees below zero, and you stop to catch your breath, your skin begins to sting immediately, your whole body hurts within seconds, and your hands and feet begin to go numb (within a minute). I guess most people wouldn't like that.

Interestingly, most people can't conceive of the back-and-forth. I've been asked, "How *did* you withstand that endless, running back-and-forth? It must be like being on a treadmill." They're right. Most people would prefer prefer running on a trail over a treadmill any day. Why? Outside you have scenery, people and other things to distract you. From a mental viewpoint, it's much easier, validating the fact that sports are more mental than physical...and so are many things in the real world, including business.

With that in mind, I knew I had to address the mental conditioning, not just the physical. I had a choice to make. I could look at the freezer as a boring situation, just running back-and-forth. If I chose this perspective, I'd surely convince myself I was bored sooner than later, and then I'd be finished, falling far short of what I was likely capable of accomplishing.

> *"The muscles of confidence and discipline are two of the most important, requiring constant conditioning."*
>
> — ANTARCTIC MIKE

Or, I could see it as an advantage. One day as I was running back-and-forth, I remembered something that my hockey coach, Ed, taught me way back in 1976. I'll never forget the Thursday night practice at 623 North Hanover Street at the Ice Palace Arena, located in Allentown, PA. I was just 11 years old. We had a big game coming up that Saturday night. Ed skated up to me and said something that changed my life: "Mike, you will play the game the way you practice. If you make the practice harder, the game will go easier."

That encounter with Ed is more vivid in my mind today than the encounter I had this morning with the barista at Starbucks. I can still see Ed in his kelly green Lehigh Valley Comets hockey jacket. His dark blue baggy sweat pants. His Koho hockey stick with the black tape on the blade. And his Bauer hockey skates with rusted blades. What Ed taught me was profound.

As I was running laps in the freezer I thought, "Mike, you can choose to see this back-and-forth-59-feet at a time as really boring; something you have to do. Or, thinking like Ed, you can see it as an advantage and your opportunity to *make the practice harder so your game will go easier.* In other words, you can change your definition of *difficult!*

This was a huge light bulb that went off in my head, as I thought "we all have a definition of difficult that determines our limits. We have a price point that is too expensive, a gap that is too big to bridge, and a ceiling that is too high. Making the practice harder so the game will go easier is the solution to changing the definition of difficult, and you don't have to be in a freezer or be an athlete to understand and benefit from this.

Then it hit me: "Don't just *practice* here…Why not *run an entire marathon* in the freezer before I go to Antarctica!" What? Are you crazy? Run 26.2 miles in a 59-foot frozen box?

Yes! I thought, "Mike, if you can run a marathon inside this freezer, you'll nail it in Antarctica because mentally, the freezer is so much harder." I set an ambitious goal to run my first marathon in 20 years, only the second of my life, inside a freezer, 59 feet at a time. That was April, 2005.

> *"You will play the game the way you practice. Make the practice harder and the game goes easier."*
>
> — HOCKEY COACH ED

From April, 2005 to October 2005, I trained in that freezer for countless hours and miles several times a week. On the weekends, I'd spend much of my Saturday and Sunday inside the freezer. Now in October, I was prepared mentally and physically for my first marathon in 20 years. It was my opportunity to see if making the practice harder by design really would make the game go easier. It was a litmus test for my muscles, but more importantly, a litmus test for my *mental* muscles.

So here I was suited up and ready for a nearly 8 hour run; back-and-forth, back-and-forth, and back-and-forth. No music, no fanfare, no windows to the outside world. I was a prisoner inside a 59-foot frozen metal box sitting surrounded by pallets of frozen who knows what stacked to the ceiling. The only sound was the constant roaring of fans pumping in the minus 20 degree air."

To track my mileage, I couldn't use a GPS, as there's no signal inside a concrete bunker—I mean freezer. So doing the calculations, it was 59 feet up and 59 feet back, totaling 118 feet in a round trip. Dividing 5,280 (number of feet in a mile) by 118 meant I had to go back-and-forth 44 times to run one mile.

Then, to mark my progress, I put a one-gallon buckets of Dryers Ice Cream on the floor to mark one mile. Now I only needed 25 more gallon buckets, plus a small pint for the two tenths. A marathon is 26-point-2 miles.

Now, here's a little psychological game that I created for myself in order to make the distance seem shorter. I broke the numbers down into bite-size pieces. Starting with the 44 laps, I grouped them into 4 sets of 11. I told myself that the first set was only practice, so it did not count. The second set was called pre-season, so it too did not count. The third set was the only one I had to do because the fourth set was a victory lap, so it too did not count. There you have it! Out of four sets, I only had to do one set of 11 laps.

That's not too hard. Taking that concept of breaking things down into even smaller pieces, I broke the 11 sets down even further. I told myself, "I'll start with one to warm up. Now I only have to do 10. The 10 is two fives. You can do *two* of *anything!* The five is just a two, with a break in the middle and repeat the two one time. There you have it. Do you hear all the one's and two's? Anybody can do one or two of anything! Now I qualify for the first mile and can put my first ice cream bucket down.

Now I need 25.2 more buckets. —No I don't!— I'll break down the 25.2 by grouping them into units of three. Why three? Think about the phone company. Why are area codes and prefixes grouped into units of three digits? Ah, because they're much easier to remember! Okay, now I only need two more buckets, totaling three. No I don't! The *first* one is a warm up; it doesn't count. The *second* one is all I need because the *third* one is a victory lap! Now I have all three.

Following that pattern, I now grouped the threes into three threes. The first one is a warm up—it doesn't count. The *second* group of three is all I need, and the third group of three is (as you now know) a victory lap! It doesn't count. You follow the logic? Like the AT&T commercials say, "It's not complicated."

Eight-and-a-half hours later, I completed my first marathon in 20 years, inside a frozen concrete box, with just 59 feet to work with. Looking back, it really wasn't that hard, because I broke the big and seemingly impossible task into pieces small enough to mentally handle.

> *"You must become comfortable being uncomfortable."*
>
> — ANTARCTIC MIKE

I understand that you're not going to run a marathon in a freezer, but here's what it means for you: I'm convinced that too many people fail in business and fall short of what they're capable of because they get overwhelmed with tasks that are much bigger or different than what they're used to. Leaders need to realize that a big part of their responsibility is to help each person figure out how to break down the task in front of them into pieces that are doable. The trick is that the pieces have to be big enough to stretch people and present a challenge. At the same time, the pieces have to be small enough so that they don't overwhelm people.

There is a balance. The work of a leader is to help each person know where that fulcrum lies on their particular balance. For every person it is different. Even if you have five people on your team who all do the same job, you have to help each one of those five individuals find the balance for what's not enough, and what's too much.

Assume they are salespeople. Let's also assume that they all have similar backgrounds in terms of experience, skill, education and motivation.

The big mistake most leaders make is to set the same expectations and strategies for each of those five people. That's not reasonable. If you do this, you'll have one person on that team who is bored, as the challenges are too small. The next person may feel like the balance is struck just right, while another will be completely overwhelmed. This is why the work of a leader is so difficult; because to do your job right, you must exert constant effort to measure, reward, challenge and set a plan for each person individually.

In summary, training in the freezer did to help me acclimate to the cold and prepare my body for what was to come. However, the real benefit of the freezer had much more to do with conditioning my *mental* muscles and teaching me two very important lessons for the real world.

One, in order to be a successful leader you have to change your definition of difficult by making the practice harder. Two, to lead people effectively, you have to help them to break down the tasks at hand into pieces that are big enough to be a challenge, but small enough to be doable. This is not easy to do and a big reason why great leadership is hard work.

> *"Ultimately, Shackleton is a success because, in him, we catch glimpses of who we want to be."*
>
> — Jonathan Karpoff

THE ANTARCTIC ICE MARATHON

Fast-forward to January 2006. All nine of us are at the starting line. We were warned by the race director that if the weather changes and gets bad, it's going to be a *mind* game, not a *physical* game. The land and the sky will mesh together, and there will be no horizon. In other words everything will be grey. Up and down, left and right, and forward from backward will all look the same. You can imagine how disoriented this would be!

The reason this could be such a mental struggle is that we could possibly be running for hours, and have no sense of forward progress, because there would be no reference point supplied by the horizon.

As soon as I heard this, my instinctive response was "Bring it on!" I began to pray for the storm of the century. A struggle like that would really be an opportunity to walk in Shackleton's shoes.

So now the race started under great weather conditions. The sun was shining brightly, the sky was solid blue, and the view on the horizon was unlimited. About a third of the way into the race, things began to change. Clouds came in and the wind picked up. Then *more* clouds came in and the wind *really* picked up. From this time forward, the winds averaged 40 to

60 miles per hour for the remainder of the race. And sure enough, up and down, left and right, and forward from backward-everything looked the same. As I struggled to determine my directions, I thought to myself "Was the path *this way, that way, or a completely different way?*"

The conclusion of the Antarctice 100K

So at this point I simply stop. I looked around. Everything was gray. The wind was howling like a freight train at more than 55 mph. The only ting I can feel is the wind tearing against my body. I look around and wondered where to go. Everything in all directions was gray. On top of that, I am alone; not a living creature in sight, and I thought, "This is exactly why I came to Antarctica!"

This was the most euphoric moment of my life and the best part of the race. I wondered, "Is this what Shackleton experienced one hundred years ago? Is this what he heard? Is this what he saw? I stared down at my footprint and wondered if anyone had ever walked in this exact spot or was I the first person to have stepped exactly in this place?

This was *really* being in the time machine—and I didn't want it to end. I felt like I was in Antarctica a hundred years ago. The date and time seemed meaningless.

I was finally able to see the path that the snowmobile had cut for the runners, and I continued on. At the 21-mile mark, our instructions were to turn around and run back to the camp. The race director had said, "When you see the tail of a DC-3 sticking up out of the ice, that's the 21-mile mark. At that point turn around and head back."

I started the final leg and then I faced a 55 mph headwind. I ran the last five miles with the wind blasting in my face. And I thought, "This-is-GREAT!" I wished that the entire race had been like this. I pushed and struggled against the wind and finally—finally—crossed the finish line.

(My time? 7 hours and 15 minutes.) Even though that was a long time, and I finished dead last, my instinctive thought was, "Is that all?" And I realized that it wasn't nearly as hard as I had thought it would be. Why? Because I had made the practice so hard in the freezer, that the game did go easier. I had redefined "difficult." I changed my definition of a marathon. Even thought I'd struggled through 55 mph winds, it wasn't that hard compared to the practice that I had intentionally made harder.

The only way I knew my time was because Richard Donovan, the race director, shouted it out. I had no idea of my time. I didn't bother to wear a watch or carry a GPS. I couldn't even tell the time of day by the sun because it hadn't set for an entire week. Due to the time of the year and how far south Antarctica is, the sun never sets at this time of year. It just goes around in circles in the sky for weeks. Noon looks exactly like midnight.

Even though I finished dead last, I was a Gold Medal winner. I felt like an Olympic champion. I had done it! I walked in the shoes of Shackleton. I got a small taste of the mental, emotional, physical and financial struggles that the Polar explorers faced 100 years ago. I had changed my definition of difficult. It was one of the most meaningful moments of my life.

GOLD MEDAL

If you've ever competed in a race, you know that one of the most common questions that people will ask you is, "What was your time?" Sure enough, upon my return from my trip to Antarctica, a friend said to me, "Wow, a marathon in Antarctica! What was your time?"

I looked at him in bewilderment and and was perplexed. "Really? *Really?!* My *time?* You know I went halfway to the moon to run this thing, right? I lived in a freezer for 10 months preparing for this. *Time??* Let me tell you about time. Seven hours and ten minutes. I finished dead last, almost an hour behind the second slowest guy."

Actually, I had been hoping to get lost and struggle out on the Polar plateau for 24 hours. Let me explain: I didn't choose to run this marathon in order to go fast—the way most runners do. In fact, running this marathon wasn't even about sports for me. It was about walking in the shoes of my hero Shackleton. For me, it was an opportunity to participate in the struggle that he experienced a hundred years ago. There was a part of me that wanted to get lost— because it was an opportunity to really share in those struggles—and to feel what they felt, see what they saw, and experience what they experienced. So actually, the longer I was out in the frozen wasteland, the better. It was more time in the time machine.

However, let's be fair to the other runners. I was one of nine people there. Two of the runners—one from Russia and one from Ireland—were there for one reason: To win. Whether it took one hour, five hours or 5 weeks didn't matter. It was about winning. Two of the other runners were there for a specific time. Where they placed did not matter; whether it was in first, the middle or last. It was about their personal time.

One woman came for another reason. She was one of two women in the race. She came to be the first woman in history to have run a marathon on all seven continents—and she won her personal Gold Medal: At 59 years old, a gal from Wales named Stevie Matthews, achieved her dream of becoming the first female runner in history to run a marathon on all seven continents of the world.

Then you have this guy from San Diego—who looks like Kenny from South Park in his red parka. He loves to hang out in freezers and wanted to get lost. So what you have here is a situation that is much like the business world. All the runners (employees) are running (working) toward the same finish line (goals of the company). However, the reasons as to why they will all finish differ significantly. While all have a desire to finish, the desire that drives one is meaningless to the next. In other words, everybody has a different definition of a Gold Medal.

What is YOUR definition of a Gold Medal?

If I had hired an Olympic-level running coach to help me prepare for Antarctica, and he didn't know how I defined my Gold Medal, he would have assumed that I was in the race to run fast and win. His approach to training me would have been a "Faster-faster! Harder-harder!" philosophy. "C'mon Mike! One more hour in the freezer will enable you to shave one minute off your time!" If he didn't know how I defined my Gold Medal, his plan would have been meaningless to me. Even if this guy had a track record of coaching Olympic Gold medalists, unless he knew how his athletes define *their* Gold Medals, all his efforts would be for naught.

He could never guess that a guy's reason for running a marathon in Antarctica was to follow in the footsteps of his Polar hero, Ernest Shackleton. In order for him to lead and engage me as my coach, he would have to know how Antarctic Mike defines *his* Gold Medal.

Then his approach to coaching me would be completely different. He would say things like, "C'mon Mike! One more hour in the freezer, and you're one step closer to following in Shackleton's footsteps. When you've walked in Shackleton's shoes you'll tell the story with more conviction. When you tell the story with more conviction, the message written on the minds and hearts of everyone who hears you will be more indelible. And when it's more indelible, people are more likely to remember and use what you taught them!" You get the point.

How much do you think this would motivate me to train harder and longer in the freezer? A whole lot… because now I'm being coached by someone who really understands how I tick, and how I define my Gold Medal.

Okay, let's transpose this onto the real world. I speak to a lot of companies all around the world, one of which is FedEx, in Memphis, Tennessee. I'm a regular there. I speak four times a year as a part of their executive curriculum. Their program puts the next line of leaders through a series of courses to help them understand how to lead before the responsibility is given to them.

One of the things I do for FedEx and other clients—in light of the importance of leaders understanding how their people define their Gold Medals—is that I make custom medals for them. So I sent the FedEx Services logo to a firm that makes custom promotional items. I designed a custom medal with a purple-and-black ribbon just for them. On the medal, I stamped "FedEx Purple Promise Ultramarathon."

The "Purple Promise" is a very important part of the FedEx culture. It's a creed that Fred Smith started when he founded the company back in 1971. Fred expected every single FedEx employee to make a commitment every day that they would make what he calls every "FedEx experience" an outstanding one. Every encounter, phone call, text message, service call, customer call, or any interaction with another employee or customer. This is the Purple Promise that he expects everyone to commit to daily. It's a huge part of their culture, and it's one of the keys to why FedEx has built a solid reputation as a great employer to work for.

So, I made these custom medals and ordered 100 of them, enough to give one to each person in my audience. After passing them out, I asked the group, "Why are you running this race? What is driving you to start and finish the Purple Promise Ultramarathon?" And I waited. The room was silent for a long time.

Then a gal named Amanda (an 18-year veteran of FedEx) raised her hand. She stood up and said, "Well, I love my boss, my job and my company. And it's important for me to save for retirement."

I looked at Amanda and said, "Thank you. But I wonder if there's something more. What do you *really* want for all this work you've put in over the past 18 years?"

Amanda hesitated then said, "I'm saving to buy a horse farm."

I said, "Tell us more about this horse farm."

She continued, "It's not just *any* horse farm. It will be a place where we give horse rides to kids who have autism. You see, I volunteer at an autism camp, and I've seen firsthand how these animals make a difference in the lives of the kids living with this condition. And with an extra sense of vigor Amanda said, "And *that's* why I'm running the Purple Promise Ultramarathon."

She sat down. A short—almost reverent—silence followed. It was a powerful moment for everyone.

After the program I asked her boss, "Did you know this about Amanda?"

He said, "I didn't have a clue."

I said, "Here's the $64,000 question: Now that you know how Amanda defines her Gold Medal, how will this help you to be a better leader and engage her more in what she does for a living here at FedEx?"

What is YOUR definition of a gold medal?

His reply was spot-on. "I don't know, but I better figure it out. She will start the race for many reasons—but she will only finish the race for *her* Gold Medal. She won't push through the difficulties for Fred's medal, for Wall Street's medal, or the medal that I think she should be running for. She'll only finish for *her* medal."

Bingo!

All of us are running our own race—doing what we do everyday in our professions. And we will only put forth our best efforts if we are running for *our own* Gold Medal.

The key questions for *you* are:

What is the definition of your *Gold Medal?*
Why are you really *running the race you've signed up for?*

Once you understand this, look out! You will run with endurance, vigor and confidence like you've never run before. Equally important, do the people on your team know the definition of their Gold Medal? When people come to grips with why they are running the race, it's amazing how they can run much further than they think they can. This is not an easy question to answer, as people and priorities change over time. Helping people to know how they define their Gold Medal and incorporating this into what they do every day is one of the most impactful things leaders can do for their team to find, engage and keep the best people.

THE BEGINNING

This is the end of the book, but it's the *beginning* of your expedition. To conquer Antarctica, literally, as an adventurer or athlete, takes months, even years. To conquer Antarctica metaphorically, as a leader, takes a lifetime. The adventure never ends, as you're called to lead every day.

And so, now that you've learned to lead at 90 degrees below zero, here are some important questions to ask yourself:

- Have I defined exactly what my Gold Medal is?

- Do I have a plan for discovering how each of my teammates defines their Gold Medal?

- Have I highlighted sections in this book that are most important to me?

- Are there any ships that I am trying to saw out of the ice? Is my team sawing away at something pointlessly?

- Which photo of Shackleton's Endurance Expedition should I hang on my wall?

- Am I committed to following in Ernest Shackleton's footsteps? (However I personally define that in my work and my life.)

GO FORTH AND CONQUER YOUR OWN ANTARCTICA!

ACKNOWLEDGMENTS

To Greg Godek, my editor and more. Thank you for blindly insisting that I go to Antarctica and run in the marathon to follow in Shackleton's shoes. I could never repay you for what you and Karyn have done for me.

To George Hubbard from SCI, the best boss I ever worked for, and for allowing me to discover Ernest Shackleton and bring his story to the leaders at SCI.

To Joni McPherson, McPherson Graphics. For 10 years you have been the most reliable and solid graphics person I could have ever found. I highly recommend you everywhere I go.

To Mark LeBlanc, NSA, for having the courage to tell me in 2006, "Oh would you just write the damn book." Well here it is Mark, just 9 years later!

To my right hand Pam Schoenfeld. You are a true lifesaver!

To David Roots, Mike Sharp and the team at Antarctic Logistics, for making my Antarctic dreams come true. You guys are the best expedition team on earth!

To Albert Martens of Winnipeg, Manitoba, for being my friend and for bringing my idea of the Polar Bear Marathon to life.

To Terri and Ted Claudett, from Quality Instant Printing, San Diego. The most reliable printers anywhere!

To Mark Beal, Brett Jewkes and the Taylor PR team for bringing Duofold into the picture and sponsoring my trips to Antarctica. You guys are the best PR team anywhere!

To Scott and BR for always having me on the air in San Diego on the best sports talk show anywhere on XX1090.

To Gerhard Sschwandtner, CEO of SellingPower for believing in me way back when.

To Jeff Zevely, KFMB, CBS 8 San Diego, for always airing my stories and believing in me. You're the best TV guy anywhere Jeff.

To Gerry Rose for being my friend and business partner on several projects. Your friendship and holding me accountable is irreplaceable.

To Bob Bortz, Lisa Seigler, Vickie Engelman and the team at FedEx Services for trusting me enough to be part of your leadership development team and the PSP program.

To Bob Perkins, Larry Reeves and the AA-ISP team for being the best sales association on the planet!

To Ned Frey, Vistage Chair, for bringing me into

Vistage. Ned, you believed in me as a speaker when few people did.

To Dana and Ellen Borowka of Lighthouse Consulting, and Gary Reuben from UCLA, for always promoting me and my story.

To Blaine Wease from the Provincial Development Group, Nashville, for having me at the Nashville Leadership Luncheon.

To Barry Trotz, Head Coach of the Washington Capitals, for having me and Angela speak to your team. Having Angela tell her story meant more to me than any moment in my career. I'll always be indebted to you Barry.

To all my friends at Vistage and TEC/TEC Canada, including but not limited to Mike Richardson, Mike Malone, David Lazzara, Ned Rowe, Sterling Lanier, David Farrington, Clyde Horner, Bob Moore, Mark Ramirez, Lance Descourouez, Richard Bell, Garth Jackson, Pat Hyndman, Rod Johnson, Niels Johnson-Lameijer, Patty Vogan, Tom Morgan, Will Henrickson, Clayton Schwerin, Loren Armenti, Conrad Prusak, Troy Smith, Pat Maley, Bob Dabic, Janet Fogarty, Bob Carrothers, Jean Maxwell, Christiaan Vandenberg, Marv Howard, John Page, Mike Mallory, Grace Attard, Paul Martin, Wayne Serie, Dick Singer, Marty Feinberg, Roark, Roger Zingle, Ned Rowe, Joni Naugle, Don Ramage, Susan Smith, Rick Harvey, Fritz Jacobi, John Howman, Joe Faessler, Beth Adkisson, Clark Vituli Don Van

Winkle, Bob Camp, Les Smolin, Ned Frey, Chuck Smith, Ron Penland, Jim Canfield, Ken Keller, Gair Maxwell, Rick McPartlin, Jennifer Gould, Ray Levesque, Tom Hardesty, Ron Means, Nora Paller, Steve Wakeen, Cathy Fitzhenry, Tim Fulton, Julie Colbrese, Jay McDonald, Don Pierro, Shel Brucker, Jim Lucas, Michael Stensaas, Sterling Lanier, Beth Miller, Susan Germaine, Brett Pyle, Dan Wertenberg, Lisa Rios, Alan Ketzes, Trent Lee, Jon Jennings, David Chavez, Steve Johnson, Ernst Bruderer, Vistage Christy Lyras, Jed Daly, Erin McGrath, Diane McIlree, Linda Gabbard, Greg Davison, John Calea, Mark Taffet, Norma Rosenberg, Diane Drewery, Maryam Maylek, Robert Berk, Mark Taylor, John Tidgewell, Christine Spray, Phil DeVries, Hal Cherny, Clyde Horner, Frank Day, Heather Anderson, Mark Winters, Linda Nelson, Gary Lockwood, Laurie Rilquemy, Ivy Gordon, Jeff Hindman, Bob Scoville, Lori, Michele, Randy Fields, Alan Weinstein, Stan Wyner Jim Wyner, Bob Vedral, Gary Hirsch, Mark Fingerlin, David Spann, PC "Hoop" Roche, Ed McClelland, John Wallingford, Jim Heller, Ted Wolf, Bently Goodwin, Linda Hughes, Don Riddell, Randy Yost, Ben Griffin, John Dame, Jerry Carlisle, Mark Shapiro, Pierre Gosselin, Rich Knauss, Barry Goldberg, Ed Cox, Brian Foley, Patrick Lee, and so many others for believing in me enough to allow me to address your teams.

To Deja Urbanovitch, Gary Gohring, Nicole Guizar, Tom McCadden, Eric Lee, Rachel Bishop, Jenn Taylor, Glenn Jeffries, Paul Davis, Mary Hoffman,

Keith Hartman, Bob McDonnell, Kevane Coleman, and the home office team at Vistage International,

To Jeff Cogan, Sean Hill, Marty Mulford, Barry Trotz and the players on the Nashville Predators, for having me as a part of your organization in many ways.

To all my corporate customers from the past couple of years including but not limited to Glen Steady, Kim Imes and the Quadrant Team, Laura Lyke and the ICC team, Walt Singer and the ACT team, Perry Walraven at Performance Controls, Jeff Rogers and the One Accord team, Kim Canon, Steve Cooper and the team at TrueBlue, John Strawser, Jared Dieselberg at Valley Interiors, Doug Bennett at Turner Construction, John Faust at Diamond Credit Union, Nora and John Eberl at Eberl Iron Works, Buffalo, Dave Beaton at Kelton Enterprises and the Tim Horton's Buffalo Team, BBJ and the ICFA board, Steve Weitekamp and the CMSA association, John Finnessey and Mark Graham from the National Portable Storage Association, Mike Klemm and the team at Cap City Speakers, Matt Pesce and the team at Zoll Medical, Justin Bredeman from Soccer Shots, Drew Firestone and the WIKA team, Trish Kordas and the TFCU team, Ila Cipriani and the Goodwill team, Chris Duncan and the Convene Team, Gary Reuben and the L'Oreal Team, Tracy Dale and Al Steele of Trilogy Athletes, Canada, Lorianne Putzier and the team at IntegraCare, Mike Scher and Dan McCann at Frontline Selling, the best lead generators going, Ryan Kring and the MSA Board, Jim

Canfield of Renaissance Executive Forums, Scott Evans from ServiceNow, Scott Harding from FB Harding, Rockville, MD, Matt Goddard and the R2i team, Tom Lipski and the Accelerent Team, Fabian Schmahl of ThyssenKrupp, and if I forgot others, you too!

Most of all, to my wife of 25 years and my best friend anywhere, Angela Pierce, who has stuck beside me and believed in me when nobody else did. Angela, you're the best thing that ever happened to me and I love you more than you'll ever know.

BIO
ANTARCTIC MIKE

Mike Pierce, aka Antarctic Mike, speaks on leadership, consults on senior staffing issues, and runs cold weather marathons. His unique approach is how he uses Antarctica as a metaphor to illustrate a variety of business topics. His presentations create powerful memories that help his audiences remember and use what they've learned.

Antarctic Mike is one of the world's busiest speakers; he travels worldwide and averages nearly two presentations per week. In between speaking engagements he is an extreme sports enthusiast, holding several world records in endurance sports. Mike was among the first nine people to run the first Antarctic Ice Marathon (2006). His motivation was not "winning" in the conventional sense; it was to follow in the footsteps of Ernest Shackleton, one of the early Polar pioneers, and a man hailed by historians and businesspeople alike to be one of the greatest leaders of all time. Not content with this "brief" experience, Mike returned to Antarctica and became the first American to complete the grueling Antarctic Ultra Marathon, a mere 100km (62.1 miles). Mike continues to take his adventure running to the coldest parts of the world. He has completed winter marathons in Siberia, the Canadian Arctic, and was the first person to run a winter marathon on the summit of Mount Washington, home of the worst weather on earth.

Mike's programs are energetic, weaving together powerful lessons on leadership and key insights from his 20 years in the recruitment business (it's not just about finding the right people, but about engaging and keeping them).

Mike has been featured on CNN, ABC, CBS, ESPN, The Wall Street Journal, The New York Times, The Los Angeles Times, Reuters. Mike has spoken for hundreds of organizations including MetLife, FedEx, Goodwill Industries, Chevron and Vistage International. His first book has recently been published, Leading at Ninety Below Zero.

Mike holds a business degree from the University of Colorado. He resides in Encinitas, California with his very patient wife, Angela, and their two cats, Yosemite and Shackleton.

Antarctic Mike
760-805-2170
www.AntarcticMike.com
AntarcticMike@gmail.com
Search "Antarctic Mike" on LinkedIn